Microsoft
Windows 98
Step by Step

Catapult   **Microsoft** Press

PUBLISHED BY
Microsoft Press
A Division of Microsoft Corporation
One Microsoft Way
Redmond, Washington 98052-6399

Library of Congress Cataloging-in-Publication Data
Microsoft Windows 98 Step by Step / Catapult, Inc.
        p.   cm.
    Includes index.
    ISBN 1-57231-683-7
    1. Microsoft Windows (Computer file) 2. Operating systems
(Computers)   I. Catapult, Inc.
QA76.76.063M24132   1998
005.4'469--dc21   98-13999
                                                                              CIP

Printed and bound in the United States of America.

1 2 3 4 5 6 7 8 9 WCWC 3 2 1 0 9 8

Distributed in Canada by ITP Nelson, a division of Thomson Canada Limited.

A CIP catalogue record for this book is available from the British Library.

Microsoft Press books are available through booksellers and distributors worldwide. For further information about
international editions, contact your local Microsoft Corporation office. Or contact Microsoft Press International
directly at fax (425) 936-7329. Visit our Web site at mspress.microsoft.com.

Microsoft, Microsoft Press, MS, MS-DOS, Windows, and Windows NT are registered trademarks and Active Desktop,
ActiveMovie, MSN, and Outlook are trademarks of Microsoft Corporation. Other product and company names mentioned herein may be the trademarks of their respective owners.

Companies, names, and/or data used in screens and sample output are fictitious unless otherwise noted.

For Catapult, Inc.
Managing Editor: Cynthia Slotvig
Publications Support Manager: Lori Kenyon
Project Editor: Holly Knobler
Production/Layout: Carolyn Thornley, Editor;
Kristi Rasmussen; Dionne Malatesta
Writer: Karen Toast Conger
Copy Editor: Debbie Wall
Technical Editor: Jesse Brasswell
Indexer: Julie Kawabata

For Microsoft Press
Acquisitions Editor: Susanne M. Forderer
Project Editor: Laura Sackermann

Table of Contents

*Quick*Look Guide

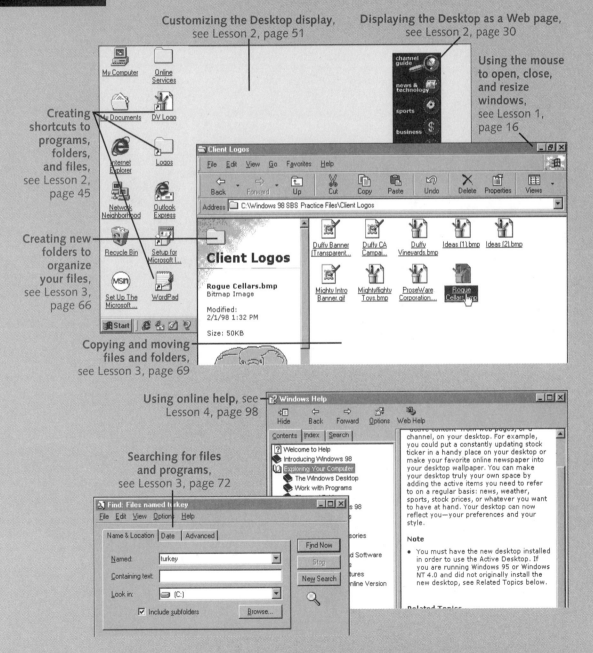

Customizing the Desktop display, see Lesson 2, page 51

Displaying the Desktop as a Web page, see Lesson 2, page 30

Using the mouse to open, close, and resize windows, see Lesson 1, page 16

Creating shortcuts to programs, folders, and files, see Lesson 2, page 45

Creating new folders to organize your files, see Lesson 3, page 66

Copying and moving files and folders, see Lesson 3, page 69

Using online help, see Lesson 4, page 98

Searching for files and programs, see Lesson 3, page 72

Customizing the Start menu,
see Lesson 4, page 89

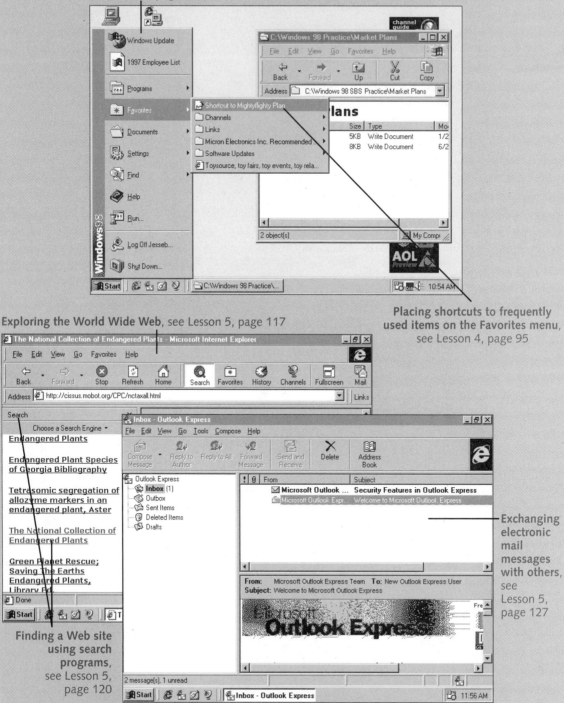

Placing shortcuts to frequently
used items on the Favorites menu,
see Lesson 4, page 95

Exploring the World Wide Web, see Lesson 5, page 117

Exchanging
electronic
mail
messages
with others,
see
Lesson 5,
page 127

Finding a Web site
using search
programs,
see Lesson 5,
page 120

Scheduling regular computer maintenance,
see Lesson 6, page 148

Using power management settings to improve energy efficiency,
see Lesson 6, page 153

Running the Accessibility Wizard,
see Lesson 6, page 154

Updating your computer with the latest additions to Windows 98,
see Lesson 7, page 168

Finding technical support documents,
see Lesson 7, page 167

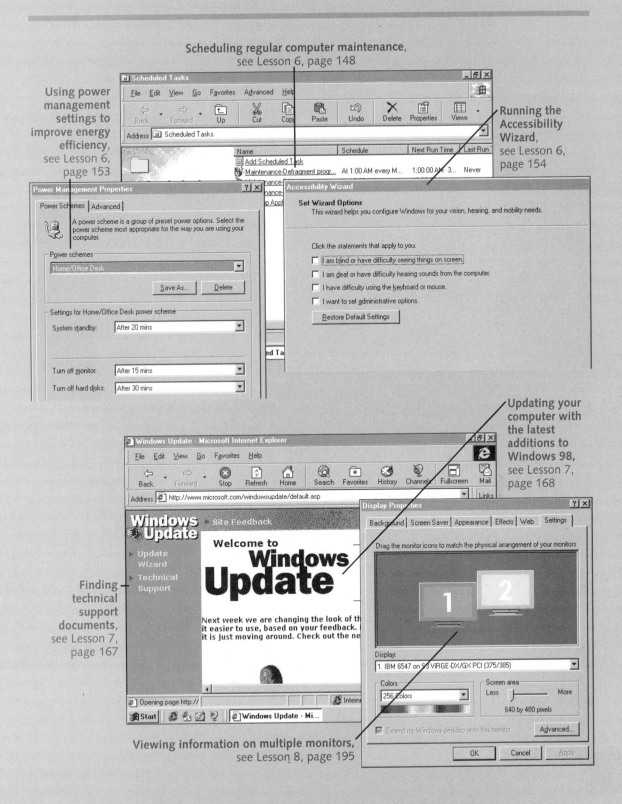

Viewing information on multiple monitors,
see Lesson 8, page 195

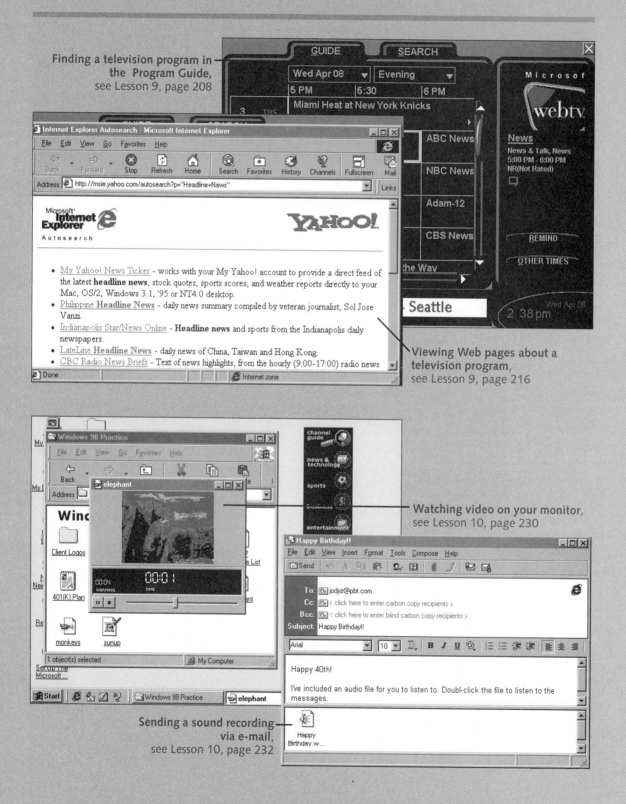

Finding a television program in the Program Guide, see Lesson 9, page 208

Viewing Web pages about a television program, see Lesson 9, page 216

Watching video on your monitor, see Lesson 10, page 230

Sending a sound recording via e-mail, see Lesson 10, page 232

Finding Your Best Starting Point

Microsoft Windows 98 is the newest Microsoft operating system for personal computers (PC's). Windows 98 expands the foundation of Windows 95 to allow you to take full advantage of new technologies in computing and entertainment. Whether you use a PC at work, at home, or both, you will find that Windows 98 is efficient, fast, and reliable. With *Microsoft Windows 98 Step by Step*, you will quickly and easily learn how to use Windows 98.

Finding Your Best Starting Point in This Book

This book is designed for beginning users of operating systems, as well as readers who have had experience with these types of programs and are switching or upgrading their current operating system to Windows 98. If you have not installed Windows 98 yet, read Appendix B, "Installing Windows 98," before proceeding. Then use the following table to find your best starting point in this book.

If you are	Follow these steps
New	
To computers	❶ Complete Lesson 1.
To graphical (as opposed to text-only) computer programs	❷ Install the practice files as described in "Using the Microsoft Windows 98 Step by Step CD-ROM."
	❸ Work through Lessons 2 through 10 chronologically.

If you are	Follow these steps
Switching From OS/2	❶ Install the practice files as described in "Using the Microsoft Windows 98 Step by Step CD-ROM." ❷ Learn basic skills for using Windows by working through Lesson 1. Then you can work through Lessons 2 through 10.

If you are	Follow these steps
Upgrading From Windows 3.1 or 3.11 From Windows 95	❶ Learn about the features of Windows 98 that are covered in this book by reading through the following section, "New Features in Windows 98." ❷ Install the practice files as described in "Using the Microsoft Windows 98 Step by Step CD-ROM." ❸ Complete the lessons that cover the topics you need. You can use the table of contentsand the *Quick*Look Guide to locate information about general topics. You can use the index to find information about a specific topic or feature.

If you are	Follow these steps
Referencing This book after working through the lessons	❶ Use the index to locate information about specific topics, and use the table of contents and *Quick*Look Guide to locate information about general topics. ❷ Read the Quick Reference at the end of each lesson for a brief review of the major tasks in the lesson. The Quick Reference topics are listed in the same order as they are presented in the lesson.

New Features in Windows 98

The following table lists the major new features of Windows 98 covered in this book and the lesson in which you can learn how to use each feature. You can also use the index to find specific information about a feature or about a task you want to perform.

The 98New icon appears in the margin throughout this book to indicate these new features of Windows 98.

New!

To learn how to	See
Upgrade to Windows 98 from other operating systems	Appendix B
View the Windows 98 Desktop as a Web page	Lesson 2
Apply the Web style to the Desktop and folders	Lesson 2
Add active content to the Desktop	Lesson 2
Customize your folders	Lesson 3
Customize your Start menu	Lesson 4
Add files, folders, and Web pages to the Favorites menu	Lesson 4
Add programs to the taskbar	Lesson 4
Subscribe to Web pages	Lesson 5
Convert to a new file allocation table	Lesson 6
Schedule automatic maintenance tasks such as ScanDisk and Disk Defragmenter	Lesson 6
Use Power Management	Lesson 6
Make the computer more accessible for people with disabilities	Lesson 6
Use the Update Wizard to update Windows 98 with the latest software additions	Lesson 7
Use Windows 98 troubleshooters to resolve conflicts	Lesson 7
Use the Disk Cleanup tool to delete files	Lesson 7
Make back up copies of your files using Microsoft Backup	Lesson 7
How to attach new Plug and Play hardware to your PC	Lesson 8
Use more than one monitor with the computer	Lesson 8
Use Web TV	Lesson 9
Use the Dial-up Connection Wizard to configure an Internet connection	Lesson 10
Use ActiveMovie to view audiovisuals	Lesson 10
Create user profiles to establish unique settings per individual computer user	Lesson 10

Corrections, Comments, and Help

Every effort has been made to ensure the accuracy of this book and the contents of the Microsoft Windows 98 Step by Step CD-ROM. Microsoft Press provides corrections and additional content for its books through the World Wide Web at http://mspress.microsoft.com/support

If you have comments, questions, or ideas regarding this book or the CD-ROM, please send them to us.

Send e-mail to:

mspinput@microsoft.com

Or send postal mail to:

Microsoft Press
Attn: Step by Step Editor
One Microsoft Way
Redmond, WA 98052-6399

Please note that support for the Windows 98 software product itself is not offered through the above address. For help using Windows 98, you can call Windows 98 Technical Support at (425) 635-7031 on weekdays between 6 A.M. and 6 P.M., Pacific Time.

Visit Our World Wide Web Site

We invite you to visit the Microsoft Press World Wide Web site. You can visit us at the following location:

http://mspress.microsoft.com

You'll find descriptions for all of our books, information about ordering titles, notices of special features and events, additional content for Microsoft Press books, and much more.

You can also find out the latest in software developments and news from Microsoft Corporation by visiting the following World Wide Web site:

http://microsoft.com/

We look forward to your visit on the Web!

Using the Microsoft Windows 98 Step by Step CD-ROM

The CD-ROM inside the back cover of this book contains the practice files that you'll use as you perform the exercises in the book and audiovisual files that demonstrate nine of the exercises. By using the practice files, you won't waste time creating the samples used in the lessons, and you can concentrate on learning how to use Microsoft Windows 98. With the files and the step-by-step instructions in the lessons, you'll also learn by doing, which is an easy and effective way to acquire and remember new skills.

important

Before you break the seal on the Microsoft Windows 98 Step by Step CD-ROM package, be sure that this book matches your version of the software. This book is designed for use with the Microsoft Windows 98 operating system. If your product is not compatible with this book, a Step by Step book matching your software is probably available. Please visit our World Wide Web site at http://mspress.microsoft.com or call 1-800-MSPRESS for more information.

Install the Practice Files

Follow these steps to install the practice files on your computer's hard disk so that you can use them with the exercises in this book.

If you are having trouble following these steps, complete Lesson 1 before installing the practice files. No practice files are needed for Lesson 1.

1. If your computer isn't on, turn it on now.

2. If you're connected to a network, you will see a dialog box asking for your username and password.

3. Type your username and password in the appropriate boxes, and click OK. If you see the Welcome dialog box, click the Close button.

Close

4. Remove the CD-ROM from the package inside the back cover of this book.

5. Insert the CD-ROM in the CD-ROM drive of your computer. In My Computer, double-click your CD-ROM drive, and then double-click the Windows 98 SBS folder.

6. Click Setup, and then follow the instructions on the screen.

   The setup program window appears with recommended options preselected for you. For best results in using the practice files with this book, accept these preselected settings.

7. When the files have been installed, remove the CD-ROM from your CD-ROM drive and replace it in the package inside the back cover of the book.

   A folder called Windows 98 SBS Practice has been created on your hard disk, and the practice files have been placed in that folder.

If your computer is set up to connect to the Internet, you can double-click the Microsoft Press Welcome shortcut to visit the Microsoft Press Web site. You can also connect to this Web site directly at http://mspress.microsoft.com

Using the Practice Files

Each lesson in this book explains when and how to use any practice files for that lesson. The lessons are built around scenarios that simulate a real work environment, so you can easily apply the skills you learn to your own work. For the scenario in this book, imagine you are a partner in the small public relations firm, ProseWare corporation. The firm specializes in designing multimedia campaigns including print, radio, and television ads for mid-sized companies. They have recently upgraded all the computers in the office from a mixture of MS-DOS, Windows 3.1, and Windows 95. You also have a computer at home running Windows 98 so you can work from home or play games.

The screen illustrations in this book might look different from what you see on your computer, depending on how your computer has been set up. To help make your screen match the illustrations in this book, please follow the instructions in Appendix A, "Matching the Exercises."

For those of you who like to know all the details, here's a list of the practice files included on the practice CD-ROM:

Filename	Description
Client Logos - folder	
Duffy Banner (Transparent)	Sample file used for sorting
Duffy CA Banner	File used in Lesson 4
Duffy Vineyards	File used in Lesson 2
Mighty Intro Banner	File used in Review & Practice 1
MightyFlighty Toys	File used in Review & Practice 1
ProseWare Corporation	File used in Lesson 2
Rogue Cellars (Transparent)	File used in Lesson 3
Rogue Cellars Label	File used in Lesson 3
Rogue Cellars	File used in Lesson 3
Rogue Cellars Logos – folder	Folder located in Client Logos folder
Clients – folder	Folder used in Lesson 3
Correspondence – folder	Folder used in Lesson 3
Garden	File used in Lesson 3
Duffy Stuff – folder	Folder located in the Correspondence folder.
F-DV Draft Marketing Plan	File used in Lesson 7
L-DV Southwest	File used in Lesson 7
Rogue Stuff – folder	Folder located in the Correspondence folder.
ToDo for Turkey Campaign	File used in Lesson 3
Market Plans – folder	
Duffy Vineyards Plan	File used in Lesson 3
MightyFlighty Plan	File used in Lesson 4 and 8
1997 Employee list	File used in Lesson 4
401(K) Plan	File used in Lesson 3
Annual Picnic Map (97)	File used in Lesson 3
Client Targets 1998	File used in Lesson 3

Filename	Description
DV Product List	File used in Lesson 3
Elephant	File used in Lesson 10
Happy Birthday	File used in Lesson 10
Monkeys	File used in Lesson 10
Sunup	Sample file used for sorting

Change the File Association for the Audiovisual Files

Throughout this book, you will see camcorder icons for audiovisual files for particular exercises. To view the audiovisual files at their best quality, you need to change the file association for the audiovisual files. The files on your computer are associated with programs. When you click on a file to open it, the program that was used to create the file will open automatically and you can view your file. If you don't change the file association, you might not be able to run or view the audiovisual files properly. Use the following steps to change the file association.

1 Click the My Computer icon.

2 On the menu bar, click View and then click Folder Options.

The Folder Options dialog box appears.

3 Click the File Types tab.

4 In the Registered File Types section, click the second Video Clip option.

In the File Type Details section, you should see the extension AVI.

5 Click Edit.

The Edit File Type dialog box appears.

6 In the Actions section, click Play.

7 Click Edit.

The Editing Action For Type: Video Clip dialog box appears.

8 Click Browse.

The Open With dialog box appears.

9 Double-click Windows.

10 Scroll until you find the Mplayer file and then click Mplayer.

11 Click Open. The Editing Action For Type: Video Clip dialog box appears.

12 Click OK.

The Edit File Type dialog box appears.

⓭ Click Close.

The Folder Options dialog box appears.

⓮ Click Close.

The My Computer windows is displayed.

⓯ Close the My Computer window.

Use the Audiovisual Files

Throughout this book, you will see icons for audiovisual files for particular exercises. Use the following steps to run the audiovisual files.

❶ Insert the Microsoft Windows 98 Step by Step CD-ROM in your CD-ROM drive.

❷ On the Windows 98 taskbar, click the Start button, point to Programs, and then click Windows Explorer.

❸ In the All Folders area, click the drive D icon (or the appropriate CD-ROM drive letter).

The contents of the CD-ROM are displayed.

❹ In the Contents Of area, double-click the AVIFiles folder.

The AVIFiles folder opens.

If the Media Player control panel opens, you will need to click Play to run the AVI file.

❺ Double-click the audiovisual file you need.

Microsoft Camcorder runs the video of the exercise. After the video is finished, Camcorder closes and you return to Windows Explorer.

❻ Close Windows Explorer, and return to the exercise in the book.

Use the Microsoft Windows 98 Starts Here Demo

The Microsoft Windows 98 Step by Step CD-ROM contains a demonstration of the Microsoft Windows 98 Starts Here which is a self-paced, interactive training product for Windows 98. The Microsoft Windows 98 Start Here Demo contains audiovisual introductions, more than 30 step-by-step, video-enhanced lessons and self-assessment quizzes to help you learn to use Windows 98. For information about ordering Microsoft Windows 98 Starts Here, click the Information link at the top of the demonstration window.

❶ Place the Microsoft Windows 98 Step by Step CD-ROM in your CD-ROM drive.

❷ Click the My Computer icon.

The My Computer window opens.

❸ Click the drive that represents your CD-ROM drive.

The contents of the Windows 98 Step by Step CD-ROM are displayed.

❹ Click the Win98sh folder.

The contents of the Win98sh folder are displayed.

❺ Click the Start file.

The browser window opens and the Microsoft Windows 98 Starts Here Demo Web page is displayed. To learn more about the demo, click the links listed at the top of the Web page. Once you have finished using the Microsoft Windows 98 Starts Here Demo, close your browser window.

Uninstall the Practice Files

Use the following steps when you want to delete the practice files added to your hard disk by the Step by Step setup program.

❶ On the Windows 98 taskbar, click the Start button, point to Settings, and then click Control Panel.

❷ Double-click the Add/Remove icon.

The Add/Remove Programs Properties dialog box appears.

❸ Click Microsoft Windows 98 Step by Step from the list, and then click Add/Remove.

A confirmation message is displayed.

❹ Click Yes.

The practice files are uninstalled.

❺ Click OK to close the Add/Remove Programs Properties dialog box.

❻ Close the Control Panel window.

Need Help with the Practice Files?

Every effort has been made to ensure the accuracy of this book and the contents of the CD-ROM. If you do run into a problem, Microsoft Press provides corrections for its books through the World Wide Web at:

http://mspress.microsoft.com/support/

We invite you to visit our main Web page at:

http://mspress.microsoft.com

You'll find descriptions for all of our books, information about ordering titles, notices of special features and events, additional content for Microsoft Press books, and much more.

Conventions and Features in This Book

You can save time when you use this book by understanding, before you start the lessons, how instructions, keys to press, and so on are shown in the book. Please take a moment to read the following list, which also points out helpful features of the book that you might want to use.

Conventions

- Hands-on exercises for you to follow are given in numbered lists of steps (1, 2, and so on). A round bullet (●) indicates an exercise that has only one step.

- Text that you are to type appears in **bold**.

- A plus sign (+) between two key names means that you must press those keys at the same time. For example, "Press ALT+TAB" means that you hold down the ALT key while you press TAB.

- The icons on the following page are used to identify certain types of exercise features:

Icon	Alerts you to

 Skills that are demonstrated in audiovisual files available on the Microsoft Windows 98 Step by Step CD-ROM.

'98 New! New features in Windows 98.

Other Features of This Book

■ You can get a quick reminder of how to perform the tasks you learned by reading the Quick Reference at the end of a lesson.

■ You can practice the major skills presented in the lessons by working through the Review & Practice section at the end of each part.

■ You can see an audiovisual demonstration of some of the exercises in the book by following the instructions in the "Use the Audiovisual Files" exercise in the "Using the Microsoft Windows 98 Step by Step CD-ROM" section of this book.

PART 1

Working in Windows 98

1

Using the
Windows 98 Desktop

**ESTIMATED
TIME
40 min.**

In this lesson you will learn how to:

✔ *Tour Windows 98 and learn the functions of each Desktop object.*

✔ *Use the mouse to open, close, and resize windows.*

✔ *Open menus to display and execute commands.*

✔ *Use dialog boxes to change the appearance of the icons on the Desktop.*

✔ *Start, close, and switch between programs.*

Imagine you are a partner in a small public relations firm that is migrating from a variety of computer systems to Microsoft Windows 98. You have been working with an MS-DOS–based computer and must now learn how to work with a mouse and the Windows 98 environment. One of your partners volunteers to assist with the transition by introducing you to the fundamentals of Windows 98.

In this lesson, you will take a tour of the Windows 98 Desktop, and you will learn how to use the mouse. You will also be introduced to windows, learn how to change their size, and learn how to move them. Finally, you will learn how to start and close programs.

Starting and Touring Windows 98

Windows 98 has just been installed on your computer. You are ready to turn on your computer, but you are interested in knowing what happens while your computer is starting. Your partner explains that when you turn on your computer,

This lesson can be reviewed rapidly by those already familiar with either Windows 95 or Windows NT 4.0.

a start program begins a series of operations referred to as the *boot cycle*. First, a system check is run to make sure that your hardware, such as your mouse and keyboard, is attached correctly and is functioning. Then, Windows 98 starts. The length of time for the boot cycle varies depending on your hardware. However, all computer systems start quicker with Windows 98 than with previous versions of the Windows operating system.

Start the computer

1. Locate the power switch on your computer, and turn your computer on.

   The Start program runs the boot cycle.

The logon procedure differs from network to network. Consult with your local network supervisor for more information.

2. If your computer is attached to a computer network, a logon dialog box appears. Type the required username and password, and press ENTER.

   The Welcome To Windows 98 dialog box appears.

Touring the Windows 98 Desktop

Now that you've started your computer, you notice that your screen looks different. Your partner explains that when you look at the Windows 98 screen for the first time, you see new items such as the horizontal band of the taskbar along the bottom and the My Computer icon in the upper-left corner. You might also see the Welcome To Windows 98 dialog box. Another name for the Windows 98 screen is the *Desktop*. The Desktop represents your work area and, just like a desk in your home or office, the contents of the Desktop change as you work.

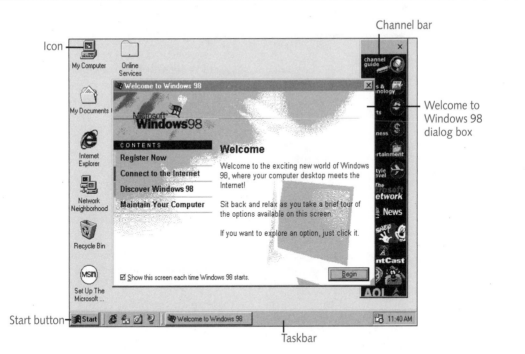

The small pictures along the left side of your Desktop are called *icons*. Icons allow you to quickly open files, folders, or programs you need. The following table provides a brief description of the Desktop icons.

Icon	Opens
	All programs, documents, and other resources available to your computer.
	A folder for the files you create.
	A browser for viewing Web pages.
	A window used to locate all the drives on your network.
	A storage location for files, folders, and other items that you have deleted, until you permanently delete them.
	A tool to assist you in setting up an Internet account on the Microsoft Network.
	A folder containing tools to assist you with creating an Internet account with major, national Internet Service Providers.
	Outlook Express, a program to send and receive electronic mail.

Using the Mouse

Now that you are familiar with the objects on the Desktop, you want to know how to use them. You tried to use your keyboard but found it awkward. You ask your partner for more help. She explains that you use a mouse for most of your work in Windows 98. She tells you that a typical mouse has two buttons: primary and secondary. Generally, the primary button is set as the left mouse button and is used for most mouse actions. The secondary button is set as the right mouse button and is used to open shortcut menus.

A mouse can have additional buttons used for programming and shortcuts. If your mouse has additional buttons, you can ignore the middle buttons while using this book. Throughout this book, reference to the left button indicates the primary mouse button while the right button indicates the secondary button.

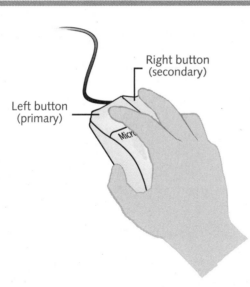

Right button
(secondary)

Left button
(primary)

The mouse is an extension of your hand, allowing you to point to, select, and control objects visible on your monitor. There are five basic actions you perform with a mouse: point, click, double-click, right-click, and drag.

When you use the mouse to point to an object, the mouse pointer shape changes. The pointer shape determines the action you can complete with the mouse. For example, a two-headed arrow indicates that the mouse pointer is positioned to resize an object. A hand with a finger pointing upward indicates that the mouse pointer is positioned over a link, or shortcut, to another file or location. After you point to an object, you are ready to perform another action. You can click, double-click, right-click, or drag the object.

When you click an object, you select it and make it active. Double-clicking an object performs the default action for the object. In computer terms, *default* means the way hardware or a program is initially set up to work. You can change some things about how most hardware and programs work. For example, you double-click the My Computer icon to open the My Computer window, and you double-click the Outlook Express icon to start Outlook Express. Right-clicking an object usually opens a shortcut menu that contains a list of commands for the object selected. Dragging an object moves the object to a new location.

Point to, select, and move objects using a mouse

You are ready to try using the mouse. In this exercise, you use the mouse to select and move an object.

1 Move the mouse until the tip of the pointer is positioned on the My Computer icon.

A ScreenTip explaining the function of My Computer is displayed.

ScreenTip

2 Click the My Computer icon by pressing and releasing the left mouse button once.

The My Computer icon changes color, indicating that it is selected for further action.

important

Be careful not to move the mouse when you are clicking an object. When you click an object and move the mouse at the same time, you move the clicked object.

3 Click the My Documents icon.

The My Documents icon changes color, indicating that it is now the active object.

④ With the mouse pointer positioned on the My Documents icon, hold down the left mouse button, drag the icon to the center of the screen, and then release the mouse button.

The My Documents icon is now located in the center of the Desktop.

⑤ Drag the My Documents icon back to its original location.

Open and close objects using the mouse

You feel comfortable pointing to, selecting, and moving objects. You are now ready to try opening windows. In this exercise, you use the double-click action to open a window, and then you close the window.

① Double-click the My Computer icon by pointing to the icon and pressing and releasing the left mouse button twice in rapid succession.

For more information on My Computer, see Lesson 2, "Customizing Your Desktop."

The My Computer window opens, and icons representing your hard disk drive, floppy disk drive, and CD-ROM drive are displayed. If the My Computer window does not open, try double-clicking faster. Be careful not to move your mouse as you double-click. You can also open the My Computer window by clicking the My Computer icon and then pressing ENTER.

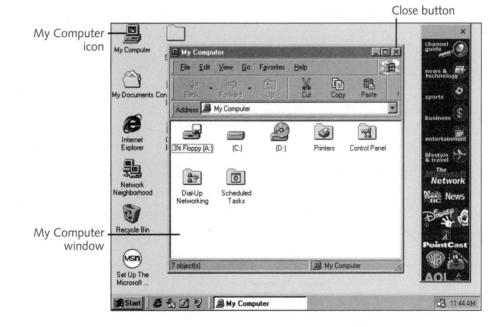

② On the My Computer window, click the Close button.
The My Computer window closes.

Close

Customizing Your Mouse

The way your mouse and mouse pointer respond to your hand and finger actions can affect your efficiency in controlling Windows 98 objects. If you are not comfortable with the default settings for your mouse, such as the double-click speed, you can change the mouse settings in Control Panel. The Control Panel is a folder that holds programs used to change and control the settings of your Desktop and program windows, mouse actions, fonts (different styles of letters, numbers, and symbols) available on your computer, network connections, modems, and so on.

Change the double-click speed setting of your mouse

1 Click the Start button in the lower-left corner of your screen, point to Settings, and then click Control Panel.

The Control Panel window opens.

2 Double-click the Mouse icon by pressing and releasing the left mouse button twice in rapid succession.

The Mouse Properties dialog box appears.

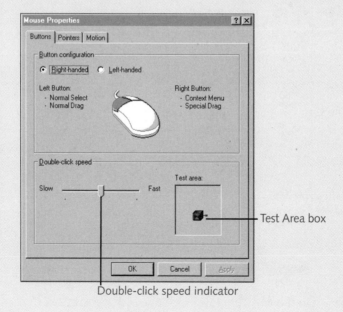

Test Area box

Double-click speed indicator

3 Double-click in the Test Area box.

The jack-in-the-box appears. If the jack-in-the-box doesn't appear, repeat step 3.

4 Drag the double-click speed indicator all the way to the left.

The double-click speed is reduced.

5 Double-click in the Test Area box.

You now can double-click at a slower speed. This means you don't have to press and release the left mouse button as rapidly.

6 Continue sampling double-click speeds until you find a comfortable speed. Then, click the OK button.

The Mouse Properties dialog box closes.

7 On the Control Panel window, click the Close button.

Displaying Menus and Commands

You ask your partner about the Start button on the taskbar. She explains that the Start button is the starting point for a session on the computer. When you click the Start button, the Start menu is displayed. You know what a menu is, but you aren't sure how it relates to your computer so you ask your partner to explain further. She tells you a *menu* is a list of commands. *Commands* are instructions you issue that tell Windows 98 to carry out an action, such as running a program, opening a document, or closing a document.

Most windows and programs have their own sets of menus and commands. For example, across the top of the My Computer window is a list of menus: File, Edit, View, Go, Favorites, and Help. This list is called the *menu bar*. If a right-pointing arrow follows a command on a menu, this means that command opens another menu. This menu is called a *cascading menu*. A cascading menu expands on the choices available to you from a single command.

Open and close menus

You are now ready to try opening and closing menus. In this exercise, you open the Start menu and a window menu.

 Click the Start button.

The Start menu is displayed.

Start menu

❷   Click a blank area on the Desktop.

The Start menu closes. You can also press the ESC key to close the menu.

❸   Double-click the My Computer icon.

The My Computer window opens.

❹   On the My Computer menu bar, click View.

The View menu is displayed.

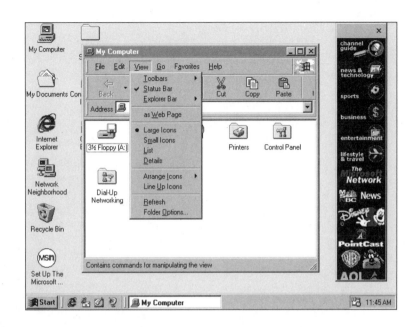

⑤   On the My Computer menu bar, click File.

The View menu closes, and the File menu is displayed.

⑥   On the File menu, click Close.

The My Computer window closes.

tip

You can activate the menu bar in a window by pressing the ALT key. When you press the ALT key, the first menu in the menu bar is highlighted. You can use the arrow keys on the keyboard to move to different menus in the menu bar, and you can press ENTER to open the selected menu.

Open a cascading menu

In this exercise, you use the Start button to open the Start menu, point to Programs, and open a cascading menu.

1   Click the Start button.

The Start menu is displayed.

2   Point to Programs.

The Programs menu is displayed to the right of the Start menu.

3   On the Programs menu, point to Accessories.

The Accessories menu is displayed to the right of the Programs menu.

4   Click the Desktop.
The menus close.

Working with shortcut menus

As you work with menus, your partner explains that you can open a *shortcut menu* by right-clicking an object or a blank area on the Desktop. Shortcut menus are context-sensitive, which means that different menus appear depending on the object or location you right-click. For example, when you right-click the Desktop, a shortcut menu listing commands to arrange icons and change Desktop properties is displayed. A shortcut menu for a file lists commands to open, delete, or rename the file.

Display shortcut menus

In this exercise, you display shortcut menus for the Desktop and the Recycle Bin.

❶ Right-click a blank area on the Desktop by pressing and releasing the right mouse button.

A shortcut menu listing commands for the Desktop is displayed.

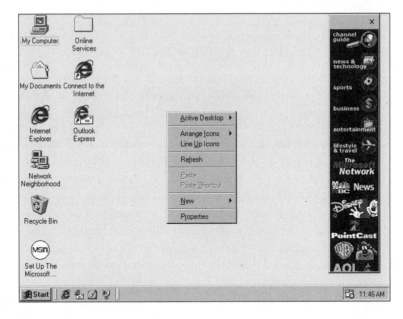

❷ Right-click the Recycle Bin.

The Desktop shortcut menu closes, and a shortcut menu listing commands for the Recycle Bin is displayed.

3   Click the Desktop.
The shortcut menu closes.

Working with Windows on Your Desktop

Your partner keeps talking about opening and closing windows, moving the window, and working with more than one window at a time. You ask her to further explain the concept of windows. Your partner tells you a *window* is a rectangular, bordered element on the Windows 98 screen. When you open a window, a button for the window appears on the taskbar and stays there until you close the window. Just as you might have several pieces of paper or file folders lying on your desk, you can have several windows open on your Desktop at the same time with each window running a different program or displaying a different document. While you can have several windows open, only one of the windows is the *active window*. An active window is the window that you are working in. When you switch to another window, that window become the active window.

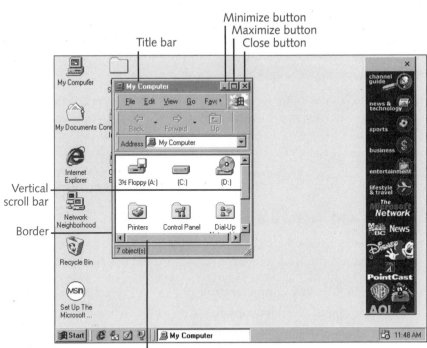

She explains that you can enlarge a window to its greatest possible size by clicking the *Maximize* button on that window's title bar. When you click the Maximize button, the window fills the entire screen and the Maximize button changes to the *Restore* button. The Restore button returns the window to the size and position it was before it was maximized.

Clicking the *Minimize* button hides the window. However, the program that was displayed in the window is still running. You can restore a minimized window by clicking the button with the window name on the taskbar.

To close a window, you click the *Close* button.

Sizing a window is useful if you have two or more windows open and would like to view them side by side. Dragging one of the borders surrounding a restored (not maximized) window changes the window's height or width. Dragging a corner simultaneously changes the height and width of the window.

If a window is large enough to display its entire contents, you only see the title bar at the top and the borders surrounding it. However, when you add more to the contents of the window or when you decrease the size of the window, portions of the window contents might become hidden. When this happens, scroll bars are displayed on the right or bottom edges of the window. You can use these bars to bring hidden portions of the window contents into view.

Maximize and restore a window

In this exercise, you use the Maximize button to see the entire contents of a window. You then use the Restore button to restore the window to its original size.

① Double-click the My Computer icon.

The My Computer window opens.

Maximize

② To see the entire contents of the My Computer window, on the My Computer title bar, click the Maximize button.

The My Computer window fills the entire Desktop. The Maximize button changes to the Restore button.

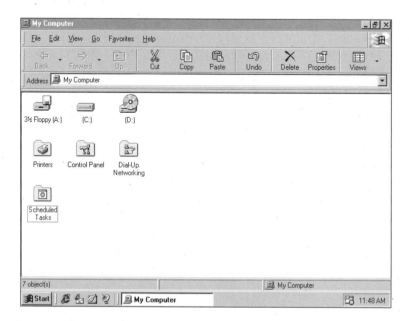

Restore

Close

3 Click the Restore button.

The My Computer window returns to its previous size and location.

4 Click the Close button.

The My Computer window closes.

Minimize and restore a window

In this exercise, you minimize a window so you can see the Desktop. You then restore the window back to its original size.

1 Double-click the My Computer icon.

The My Computer window opens.

Minimize

2 On the My Computer title bar, click the Minimize button.

The My Computer window is minimized, and its name remains on the taskbar at the bottom of the screen.

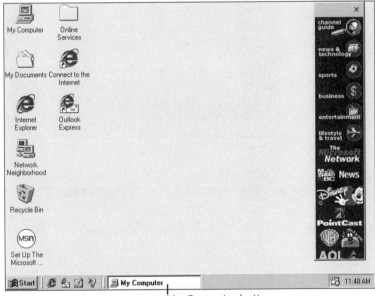

My Computer button

3 On the taskbar, click the My Computer button.

The My Computer window returns to its previous size and location.

4 Click the Close button.

The My Computer window closes.

Using the Windows 98 Desktop   1

Adjust window size

In this exercise, you change the size of a window by dragging its borders.

For a demonstration of how to change the size of a window, in the AVIFiles folder on the Microsoft Windows 98 Step by Step CD-ROM, double-click the page 20 icon.

1 Double-click the My Computer icon.

The My Computer window opens.

2 Position the mouse pointer on the right border of the My Computer window.

The pointer shape changes to a two-headed arrow pointing left and right.

3 Drag the border approximately one inch to the left to make the window narrower.

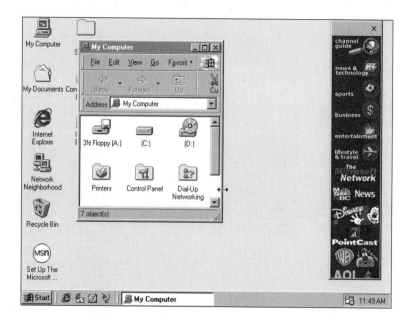

4 Drag the border back to the previous position.

5 Point to the lower-left corner of the My Computer window.

The pointer shape changes to a two-headed diagonal arrow.

6 Drag the border diagonally, approximately one inch upward and one inch to the right.

The window size changes in the direction that you just dragged.

7 Drag the border back to the previous position.

8 Click the Close button.

Close

Use scroll bars to reveal hidden window contents

In this exercise, you resize a window to display scroll bars. You then use the scroll bars to display different portions of the window contents.

1 Double-click the My Computer icon.

The My Computer window opens.

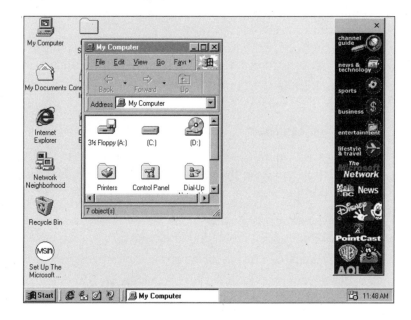

2 Double-click the Control Panel folder.

The Control Panel folder opens.

3 Drag the right border to the left approximately two inches.

Vertical and horizontal scroll bars are displayed on the Control Panel window.

4 On the vertical scroll bar, click the down arrow twice.

The other icons in the Control Panel window come into view.

5 On the horizontal scroll bar, click the light gray scroll bar area to the right of the scroll box.

More icons in the Control Panel window come into view.

6 Drag the horizontal scroll box to the left.

The objects that were hidden are now displayed.

7 Drag the borders of the Control Panel window until the window is close to the size it was when you first opened it.

8 Click the Close button.

Working with the Taskbar and Dialog Boxes

See Lesson 2, "Customizing Your Desktop," for more information about channels.

After your tour of the Desktop and introduction to using a mouse and controlling windows, your partner shifts your attention to the taskbar. She has already mentioned that the taskbar is a rectangular bar that runs horizontally across the bottom of your screen and that it contains the Start button. She continues by pointing out that you can use the taskbar to quickly switch between open windows. When you minimize a window, a button for that window remains displayed on the taskbar. You can view the window by clicking the button. She also points out the four icons next to the Start button. She explains that you can use the four icons to quickly start your Internet browser, start Outlook Express, minimize all open windows at once, or view your channels. You can also move your taskbar to either side or to the top of your Desktop.

Move the taskbar

In this exercise, you move the taskbar to the top of the Desktop by using your mouse to drag and drop the taskbar. You then move the taskbar to the left side of the Desktop.

 Move your mouse pointer to the taskbar, press and hold down your left mouse button, and then drag the taskbar to the top of the Desktop.

Your taskbar is now displayed at the top of the screen.

❷ Move your mouse pointer to the taskbar, press and hold down your left mouse button, and then drag the taskbar to the left side of the Desktop.

Your taskbar is now displayed on the left side of your Desktop.

Specifying options in dialog boxes

While you've been working with menus, you realize that some of the Windows 98 commands you choose require more information from you before they can be carried out. For instance, to change the taskbar display properties, Windows 98 needs specific information about how you would like the taskbar to appear. You ask your partner about this and she tells you that you use dialog boxes to enter more information. *A dialog box* displays areas in which you select or enter the required additional information. A dialog box cannot be maximized or minimized. After you type in the necessary information, Windows 98 can continue to carry out your command.

Use a dialog box to change the icons on the Start menu to small icons

In this exercise, you use the Taskbar Properties dialog box to change the icons on the Start menu to small icons.

1 Right-click a blank area on the taskbar.

A shortcut menu is displayed.

2 On the shortcut menu, click Properties.

The Taskbar Properties dialog box appears.

3 On the Taskbar Options tab, select the Show Small Icons In Start Menu check box.

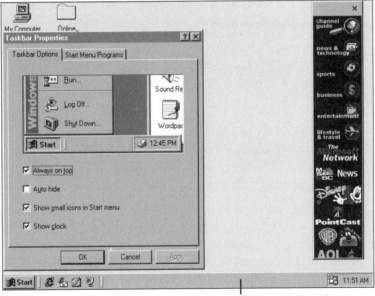

Blank area of taskbar

4 Click the OK button.

The Taskbar Properties dialog box closes.

View the change to the Start menu

In this exercise, you view the results of the previous exercise by looking at the Start menu to see the small icons.

1 Click the Start button.

The Start menu is displayed.

Using the Windows 98 Desktop 1

2   Click a blank area on the Desktop.

The Start menu closes.

Use the dialog box to change the icons on the Start menu to large icons

In this exercise, you use the Taskbar Properties dialog box to change the icons on the Start menu to large icons.

1   Right-click a blank area on the taskbar.

A shortcut menu is displayed.

2   On the shortcut menu, click Properties.

The Taskbar Properties dialog box appears.

3   Clear the Show Small Icons In Start Menu check box.

The option is cleared.

4   Click the OK button.

Starting and Closing Programs

Your partner has been helping you learn Windows 98 and how to use some of the features. Next you want to learn how to start and close programs. She explains that Windows 98 includes many programs designed to help you perform various tasks with your computer. In addition, most software programs add a command to the Programs menu when they are installed.

Your partner tells you that when you start a program, a button for the program window is displayed on the taskbar. This button shows you which program is open and allows you to switch from one program window to another. If open windows obscure the Desktop contents, you can use the Show Desktop icon on the taskbar to minimize all open windows, allowing a clear view of the Desktop.

Start programs from the Start menu

In this exercise, you start the WordPad program. Then, you start the Paint program. You can create documents, such as a letter or memo, in WordPad and use Paint to draw maps and pictures.

1   Click the Start button.

The Start menu is displayed.

2   Point to Programs, and then point to Accessories.

The Accessories menu is displayed.

3 Click WordPad.

The WordPad program starts, and the WordPad window opens.

4 Click the Start button.

The Start menu is displayed.

5 Point to Programs, and then point to Accessories.

The Accessories menu is displayed.

6 Click Paint.

The Paint program starts, and the Paint window opens. Both WordPad and Paint are open on the Desktop.

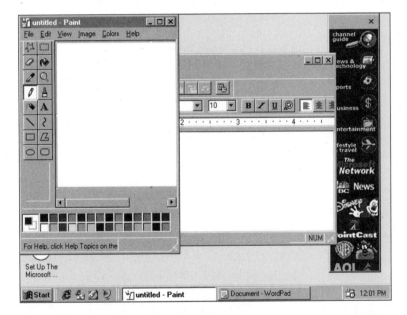

Switch between programs using the taskbar

In this exercise, you switch between WordPad and Paint using the buttons on the taskbar. You also minimize both programs by using the Show Desktop icon on the taskbar.

1 Be sure that WordPad and Paint are open on the Desktop. On the taskbar, click the WordPad button.

WordPad becomes the active window.

Show Desktop

2 To see the entire Desktop, on the taskbar, click the Show Desktop icon.

Both the Paint and WordPad windows are minimized, showing the entire Desktop.

❸ On the taskbar, click the Paint button.

The Paint window is restored.

❹ Close the Paint window and the WordPad window.

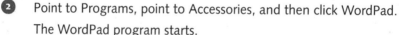

tip

You can switch rapidly between programs using the ALT and TAB keys. Press and hold the ALT key while simultaneously pressing the TAB key once. A window with an icon representing each open window is displayed. Continue to hold down ALT and press TAB again. A different icon is selected. Continue to hold down ALT and press TAB until you have selected the icon you want. Release both keys.

Close programs

In this exercise, you close WordPad using a command on a shortcut menu. Then you close Paint using the Close button.

❶ Click the Start button.

❷ Point to Programs, point to Accessories, and then click WordPad.

The WordPad program starts.

❸ Minimize the WordPad window.

❹ Click the Start button.

❺ Point to Programs, point to Accessories, and then click Paint.

The Paint program starts.

❻ On the taskbar, right-click the WordPad button.

A shortcut menu is displayed.

❼ On the shortcut menu, click Close.

The WordPad program closes.

❽ On the Paint window, click the Close button.

The Paint program closes.

Shutting down Windows 98

You look at the clock on the taskbar and realize that your workday has ended. You want to turn off your computer and go home. Your partner walks into your office to say goodnight and notices you are about to press the power button on your computer. She stops you and explains that if you just turn off your computer while Windows 98 is still running, you could lose data. Instead, she tells you to use the Shut Down command on the Start menu.

Shut down Windows 98

In this exercise, you use the Start menu to shut down Windows 98.

1 Click the Start button and then click Shut Down.

The Shut Down Windows dialog box appears.

2 Select the Shut Down option.

3 Click OK.

Windows 98 shuts down, and a message informing you it is now safe to turn off your computer is displayed.

Newer computers will turn off automatically.

4 Turn off your computer.

Lesson 1 Quick Reference

To	Do this	Button
Click an object	Point to the object, and then press and release the left mouse button.	
Right-click an object	Point to the object, and then press and release the right mouse button.	
Double-click an object	Point to the object, and then press and release the left mouse button twice in rapid succession.	
Drag an object on the Desktop	Point to the object, hold down the left mouse button, move the mouse pointer to a new location, and then release the mouse button.	
Open a menu	Click the menu name.	
Open a cascading menu	Point to a menu command that is followed by a right-pointing arrow. Click the menu name or button.	
Close a menu	Click a blank area on the Desktop.	
Open a shortcut menu for an object	Right-click the object.	
Run a command on a menu	Click the command.	
Maximize a window	Click the Maximize button on the window's title bar.	

Using the Windows 98 Desktop 1

Lesson 1 Quick Reference

To	Do this	Button
Restore a maximized window to its former size	Click the Restore button on the window's title bar.	
Minimize a window	Click the Minimize button on the window's title bar.	
Restore a minimized window to its former size and location	Click the window's button on the taskbar.	
Resize a window	Drag one of the window's borders or corners.	
View hidden contents in a window	Drag the scroll box. *or* Click the scroll	
Close a window	Click the Close button on the window's title bar.	
Start a program	Click Start. Point to Programs. Click the program name.	
Switch between programs	Click the program name on the taskbar. *or* Hold down ALT and press TAB. While continuing to hold down ALT, press TAB until you select the icon for the program you want to open. Release both keys.	

2

Customizing Your Desktop

**ESTIMATED
TIME
40 min.**

> ### In this lesson you will learn how to:
>
> ✔ *Change the Desktop and folders to work more like a Web page.*
> ✔ *Place items on the Desktop that display current information such as weather or news.*
> ✔ *Use shortcuts to open programs, folders, and files quicker.*
> ✔ *Customize your Desktop by changing colors, background, and screen savers.*

Your firm has finished the upgrade to Microsoft Windows 98. Now you want to personalize your Desktop and change the way Windows works so that your environment is the most comfortable for you.

In this lesson, you will learn how to personalize the Windows 98 Desktop. You will change the Desktop and folders to function more like a Web page. You will add *active content* windows that search the Internet for current news, and you will create shortcuts that speed the opening of frequently used files and programs. You will also implement cosmetic changes to the desktop colors, background, and screen saver.

Introducing Active Desktop

Active Desktop lets you put active content from the World Wide Web on your Desktop. Active content is information from the Web that constantly changes.

For example, if you like to see how your stock is doing, you can add a stock ticker to your Desktop so you can keep track of your stock. The stock ticker is constantly updated with information from the Web.

Your firm plans to start aggressively using the World Wide Web to conduct business. With Active Desktop, you can make the Desktop function more like a Web page. You can then use the same techniques to work with files and programs on your own computer as you use with information on the Web.

The first change you notice when you view the Desktop as a Web page is the appearance of the channel bar. The channel bar is a series of buttons that provide immediate access to World Wide Web sites. As your needs change, you can hide or display the channel bar. Another change you can make when you view the Desktop as a Web page is to change folder options so that you can open windows, files, or folders with a single click, instead of a double click.

After recognizing that your firm is using the Web more and more, you decide to take advantage of the Active Desktop feature that makes the Desktop look more like a Web page.

View the Desktop as a Web page

The following exercises start with the View As Web Page option disabled and the Classic Style folder options enabled.

In this exercise, you change your Desktop to view it as a Web page.

1. Right-click a blank area on the Desktop.

   A shortcut menu is displayed.

2. Point to Active Desktop, and then click View As Web Page.

   The View As Web Page option is selected, and the channel bar appears as a vertical band on the right side of the monitor.

Close the channel bar

The channel bar takes valuable space on the Desktop that some would like to use for icons. In this exercise, you close the channel bar.

❶ Be sure that the View As Web Page option is selected. Point to the top of the channel bar.

A gray band appears at the top of the channel bar.

Close

❷ Click the Close button.

The channel bar closes. It will remain closed until you display it.

Display the channel bar

❶ Right-click a blank area on the Desktop.

A shortcut menu is displayed.

❷ Point to Active Desktop, and then click Customize My Desktop.

The Display Properties dialog box appears.

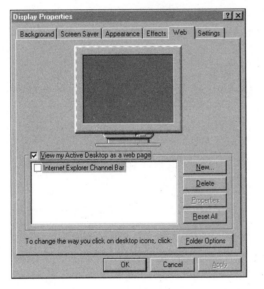

❸ Select the Internet Explorer Channel Bar check box.

The channel bar is displayed in the upper portion of the dialog box.

④ Click OK.

The channel bar is displayed. The channel bar will remain displayed until you close it.

Apply the Web style to your Desktop and folders

① Right-click a blank area on the Desktop.

A shortcut menu is displayed.

② Point to Active Desktop, and then click Customize My Desktop.

The Desktop Display Properties dialog box appears.

③ Click the Folder Options button.

A message asking if you want to close the Display Properties dialog box and view the Folder Options dialog box instead is displayed.

④ Click Yes.

The Folder Options dialog box appears, and the General tab is active.

⑤ In the Windows Desktop Update area, select the Web Style option, and click OK.

The Single-Click dialog box appears.

⑥ Click the Yes option, and click OK.

The Single-Click dialog box closes, and the icons on the Desktop are underlined, which indicates that they can be opened with a single click rather than a double click.

Select and open objects in Web style display mode

You have changed your folder options to Web style, and you decide to practice opening objects using a single click. In this exercise, you open My Documents using the single-click method.

1 Be sure that the Web Style option is selected. Point to the My Computer icon.

The mouse pointer changes to a hand as it moves over the icon. The My Computer icon changes color, which indicates that it is selected.

Hand over My Computer

Underlined icons

2 Click the My Computer icon.

The My Computer window opens.

Close

3 Close the My Computer window.

Customizing Your Desktop 2

Using the My Computer Icon to Learn More About Your Files and Folders

The remainder of this book assumes that you are viewing the Active Desktop as a Web page with the Web Style option selected.

As your client base grows, you create and save many files. To view these files, you use the My Computer icon. Clicking the My Computer icon displays the contents of your computer. You can browse through files, organize your work into folders, or copy files from one location to another.

When you first open the My Computer window, you see a group of icons. Each icon represents either a drive or a folder. When you click a drive icon, the contents of the drive are displayed in the My Computer window. For example, when you click the drive C icon, the contents of your hard disk are displayed. Alternatively, if you click the Control Panel folder, then the contents of the Control Panel folder are displayed.

When you point to an icon in the My Computer window, information about the icon is displayed on the left side of the My Computer window. For example, when you point to the drive C icon, the size of your hard disk and the amount of free and used storage space is displayed. If you point to the Control Panel icon, a short description of its contents and function is displayed.

One of your partners is going on extended leave. He has asked you to take over several of his accounts. You need to transfer his files to your computer, but you are not sure if you have enough space on your hard disk.

View drive and folder information

In this exercise, you view information about your hard disk and the Control Panel folder.

 1 Click the My Computer icon.

The My Computer window opens.

Maximize

2 To see all the contents in the My Computer window, click the Maximize button on the My Computer title bar.

3 Point to the drive C icon.

The My Computer window splits and information about drive C is displayed in the left pane. The contents of My Computer are displayed in the right pane. You can use the scroll bar between the two panes to view additional information about My Computer.

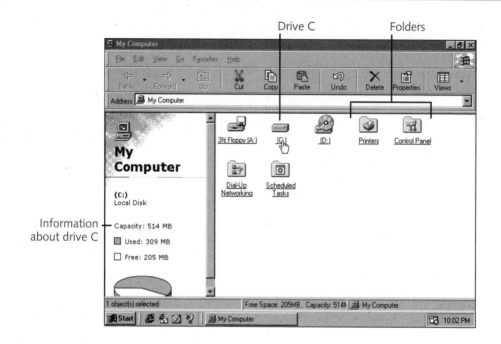

④ Point to the Control Panel folder.

Information about the function of the Control Panel is displayed in the left pane.

⑤ Close the My Computer window.

Viewing the contents of drives and folders

Because disks can store such large quantities of information, it is useful to organize the information in folders. A *folder* is a container in which documents, program files, and other folders are stored. Folders allow you to separate materials by function or topic. A folder within a folder is referred as a *subfolder*.

When you click a folder, the My Computer window changes to display the contents of the folder. Each time you click a folder, the address bar changes to reflect your new location. Every location and file is identified by a unique address. If you know the exact address for a folder or file, you can type it into the address bar. In this way, you can skip from one location to another without clicking through the intervening steps.

The Back, Forward, and Up One Level buttons on the toolbar are useful in browsing folders and files. Windows 98 maintains a history of locations you view. The Back button moves you backward page by page through the list of locations you have visited. The Forward button moves you forward page by page through the locations you have visited. The Up One Level button displays the disk or folder that contains the folder you are currently viewing. For example, if you are viewing the Windows folder and click the Up One Level button, the contents of drive C are displayed.

One of the senior partners in your firm has just retired. You have been given several folders and files created for a group of clients, and you want to know what the folders contain.

Display folder contents on your hard disk using the mouse and navigator buttons

In this exercise, you use the mouse and navigator buttons in the My Computer window to explore the contents of folders.

❶ Click the My Computer icon.

❷ Click the Maximize button on the My Computer title bar, and click the drive C icon.

The Drive C window opens.

❸ Click the Windows 98 SBS Practice folder.

The Windows 98 SBS Practice folder opens.

❹ Click the Client Logos folder.

The Client Logos folder opens.

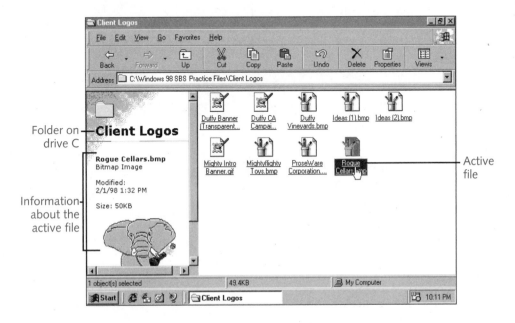

Folder on drive C

Information about the active file

Active file

Back

5 To see the contents of the Windows 98 SBS Practice folder, click the Back button.

The contents of the Windows 98 SBS Practice folder are displayed. The Windows 98 SBS Practice folder contains the Client Logos folder.

6 To see the contents of drive C, click the Back button.

The contents of drive C are displayed.

Forward

7 To see the contents of the Windows 98 SBS Practice folder, click the Forward button.

The contents of the Windows 98 SBS Practice folder are displayed.

8 Click the Up One Level button twice.

The contents of My Computer are displayed.

Up One Level

Display folder contents on your hard disk using the address bar

As you become more familiar with your folders and files, you might find that you can move more rapidly from folder to folder by typing the folder location into the address bar. In this exercise, you move directly from drive C to the Client Logos subfolder. Then you use the navigator buttons to quickly switch back and forth between drive C and Client Logos.

1 Be sure that the My Computer window is maximized. Click in the address bar. The text "My Computer" is selected.

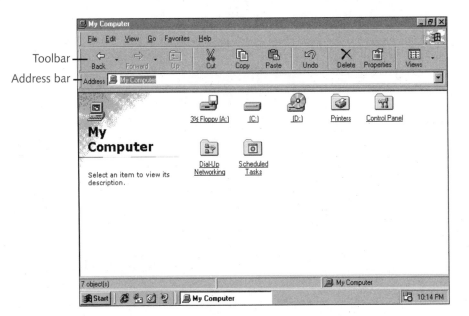

❷ Type **C:** and press ENTER.

The contents of drive C are displayed.

❸ To move directly to the Client Logo folder, click the address bar, and then type **C:\Windows 98 SBS Practice\Client Logos**

The Client Logos folder is a subfolder of Windows 98 SBS Practice. By typing the address into the address bar, you move directly from drive C to the subfolder without displaying the contents of Windows 98 SBS Practice folder. The backslashes are used to separate folders.

❹ Press ENTER.

The Client Logos folder opens.

❺ To view the contents of drive C, click the Back button.

The window display returns to drive C.

❻ Click the Forward button.

The contents of the Client Logos folder are displayed again. The Back and Forward buttons make it possible to rapidly switch between the two folders without having to open other folders.

❼ Close the My Computer window.

tip

As you type new locations in the address bar, a Windows 98 feature called AutoComplete attempts to fill in the address as you type it. AutoComplete fills in the address based on the locations you have viewed before. You can override the address that is displayed by continuing to type. If AutoComplete fills in an address that is correct, you can press the RIGHTARROW key or the END key when the desired folder name appears. The insertion point moves to the end of the address text. The insertion point is a blinking vertical bar that marks the place where text will appear when you type.

Putting Active Content Items on the Desktop

New!

By integrating the Windows 98 Desktop with the standards and technology of the World Wide Web, new possibilities emerge for connecting Web content to your computer. You can now add active content windows to your Desktop. Active content is information that is regularly updated on your screen, such as a stock ticker or a weather map. The data for active content items arrives from the Internet at regularly scheduled intervals over either a network connection or a modem.

You add active content items from Microsoft's Active Desktop Gallery, a Web page on the Internet. The Active Desktop Gallery includes pages developed by both commercial and non-profit organizations and is a convenient and reliable source of active content items.

An active content item on your Desktop has many of the same properties as a normal window. If an active content item is hidden behind the channel bar or another Desktop object, you can move the item window by dragging the title bar. You can also resize an active content item by dragging its borders. Click the Close button. The item remains on your computer, which allows you to view it again at a later date.

You are planning a business trip to Seattle and would like to keep an eye on weather conditions. You decide to add an active content weather map to your Desktop. When you select an item in the Active Desktop Gallery, the active content Web page is transferred from the Internet to your hard disk. After you place the weather map on your Desktop, you discover that some of the Desktop objects hide half of the map, so you move the map to another location. After your trip to Seattle, you find you no longer need the weather map in the middle of your Desktop. You might, however, need the map at some later date, so you close the map but don't delete it from your hard disk.

Add a new active content item to the Desktop

For a demonstration of how to connect to the Active Desktop Gallery, in the AVIFiles folder on the Microsoft Windows 98 Step by Step CD-ROM, double-click the page40 icon.

In this exercise, you connect to the Active Desktop Gallery and locate an active content item that displays a weather map of the United States. You then add the weather map item to your Desktop.

1   Right-click a blank area on the Desktop.

A shortcut menu is displayed.

2   Point to Active Desktop, and then click Customize My Desktop.

The Display Properties dialog box appears.

3   Click the New button.

The New Active Desktop Item dialog box appears.

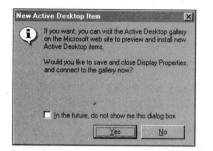

④ Click the Yes button.

The browser window opens, and the Active Desktop Gallery page appears.

Maximize

⑤ Click the Maximize button.

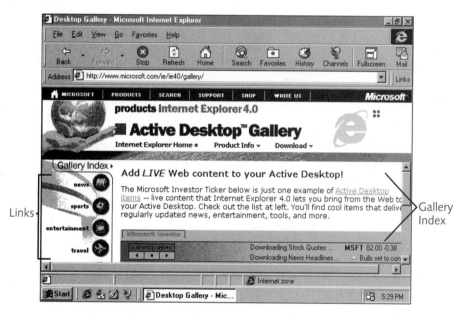

⑥ To locate the MSNBC Weather Map, scroll down and click the Weather link.

⑦ In the Gallery Index, click the MSNBC Weather Map link.

The weather map appears in the browser window.

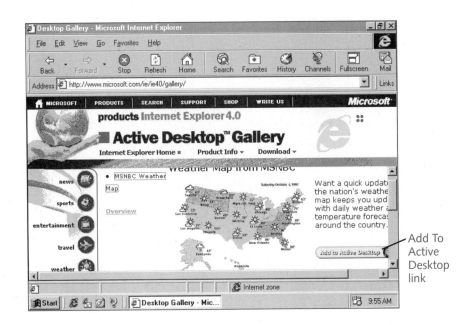

Add To
Active
Desktop
link

8 Click the Add To Active Desktop link.

A message asking if you want to add a Desktop item to your Active Desktop is displayed.

9 Click Yes.

The Add Item To Active Desktop dialog box appears.

10 Click OK.

The subscription information and Web page for the MSNBC weather map are copied to your hard disk. The weather map is displayed on your Desktop.

Minimize

11 Click the Minimize button on the browser window.

The browser window minimizes to display the Desktop, and you can see the weather map you just added to your Desktop.

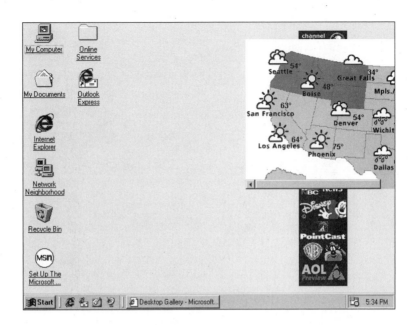

Move an active content item on the Desktop

You can move and resize active content items in the same fashion as you would any other window on the Desktop. In this exercise, you move an active content item to a more convenient location.

1   Be sure that the MSNBC weather map is displayed on the Desktop. Point to the top edge of the Weather Map window.

A gray title bar appears at the top of the item.

2   Drag the title bar to the upper-middle portion of your screen.

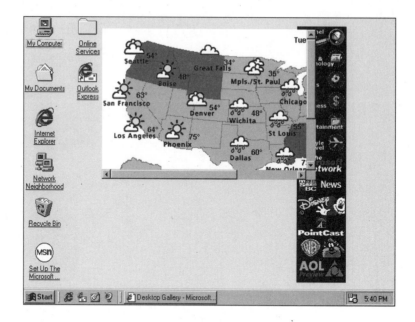

Close an active content item window

1 Be sure that the MSNBC weather map is displayed on the Desktop.

Close

2 On the Weather Map title bar, click the Close button.

The weather map closes. It will not open until you display it again.

View active content items loaded on your computer

You can copy many active content items to your hard disk and display on your Desktop only those items that are useful to you. In this exercise, you will view the list of active content items loaded on your hard disk.

1 Right-click a blank area on the Desktop.

A shortcut menu is displayed.

2 Point to Active Desktop, and then click Customize Your Desktop.

The Desktop Display Properties dialog box appears. A list of all the active content items downloaded, or transferred, to your computer is displayed. You can select the active content items you want to see by selecting the check box to the left of each active content item. If you completed the two previous exercises, the MSNBC Weather check box will be displayed. If you select the MSNBC Weather check box, the weather map active content item will appear on your Desktop.

3 Click the Cancel button.

The Display Properties dialog box closes.

Using Shortcuts to Speed Your Work

To work efficiently in your home or office, you might place on your desk the tools you use most frequently. For example, folders for current projects are within sight and a stapler and paper clips are within reach. In the same fashion, you can customize the Windows 98 Desktop with shortcuts to the files, folders, and programs important to your work.

Customizing Your Desktop   2

A *shortcut* is a pointer to a document, folder, or program. Clicking a shortcut immediately opens that document, folder, or program. Once a shortcut is placed on the Desktop, you don't need to browse through My Computer to find that file or folder. The method to create a shortcut is the same for files, folders, and programs. The name of a new shortcut is "Shortcut to" and the name of the original object. For example, a shortcut to the Duffy Vineyards Logo file is automatically named "Shortcut to Duffy Vineyards Logo." You can change the name of a shortcut at any time.

As you create shortcut icons, the Desktop can start to look cluttered. When you right-click the Desktop, a shortcut menu is displayed, which includes commands to organize icons by name, type, size, or date. These commands always organize the Windows 98 Desktop icons first and then the shortcuts you create. In other words, My Computer, My Documents, Internet Explorer, Recycle Bin, and My Briefcase are displayed on the left edge of the screen followed by personal shortcuts. You can remove the shortcuts you created by moving them to the Recycle Bin.

You start the WordPad program almost every day, and you have a client logo folder with one particular client file that you work with every day. You would like to be able to open WordPad and the folder as quickly as possible, so you decide to place shortcuts to this program and folder on your Desktop. Then you rename the shortcuts with shorter names. Finally, after you finish the project that uses the client logos, you delete the folder shortcut.

Create a shortcut to a program

In this exercise, you create a shortcut to the WordPad program and then use the shortcut to start WordPad.

 Click the Start button, point to Programs, and then point to Accessories.

❷ On the Accessories menu, right-click and drag WordPad to a blank area on the Desktop.

A shortcut menu is displayed.

❸ Click Create Shortcut(s) Here.

A shortcut icon of WordPad is displayed on the Desktop.

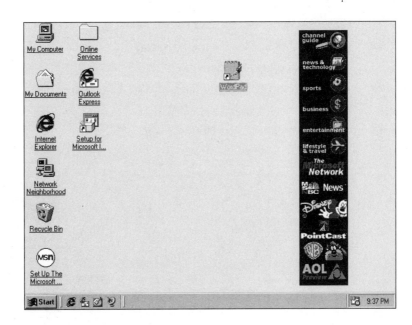

4 Click the WordPad shortcut icon.

The WordPad window opens.

5 Close the WordPad window.

Create shortcuts to a folder and file

In this exercise, you create a shortcut to the Client Logos folder on the Desktop. You also create a shortcut to a file that is stored in the Client Logos folder.

1 Click the My Computer icon.

2 Click the drive C icon, and then click the Windows 98 SBS Practice folder.

The Windows 98 SBS Practice folder opens.

3 Right-click and drag the Client Logos folder to a blank area on the Desktop.

A shortcut menu is displayed.

4 Click Create Shortcut(s) Here.

The Shortcut to Client Logos icon is displayed on the Desktop.

5   Close the Windows 98 SBS Practice window.

6   Click the Shortcut to Client Logos icon.

The Client Logos folder opens.

7   Right-click and drag Duffy Vineyards to a blank area on the Desktop.

A shortcut menu is displayed.

8   Click Create Shortcut(s) Here.

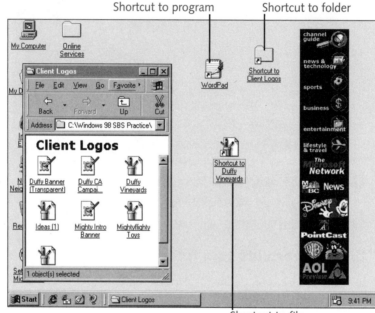

Shortcut to program   Shortcut to folder

Shortcut to file

9   Close the Client Logos window.

Rename a shortcut

When you create shortcuts, you might not be able to see the entire name under the icon or you might want to rename the shortcut to something you will remember better. In this exercise, you rename file and folder shortcuts.

1   Right-click the Shortcut to Client Logos icon.

A shortcut menu is displayed.

2   Click Rename.

The Shortcut to Client Logos text is highlighted.

3 Type **Logos** and press ENTER.

The shortcut is renamed "Logos."

4 Right-click the Shortcut to Duffy Vineyards icon.

A shortcut menu is displayed.

5 Click Rename.

6 Type **DV Logo** and press ENTER.

Use a shortcut to open a file

In this exercise, you will test a file shortcut. When you click a file shortcut, it starts the program the file was created in and opens the file.

1 On the Desktop, click the DV Logo icon you created in a previous exercise.

The Paint program starts, and the Duffy Vineyards Logo file opens.

2 Close the Paint window.

The Paint window closes.

Arrange your icons on the Desktop

In this exercise, you arrange your icons on the Desktop by name.

1 Right-click a blank area on the Desktop.

A shortcut menu is displayed.

2   Point to Arrange Icons, and then click By Name.

The icons are arranged on the left side of the Desktop.

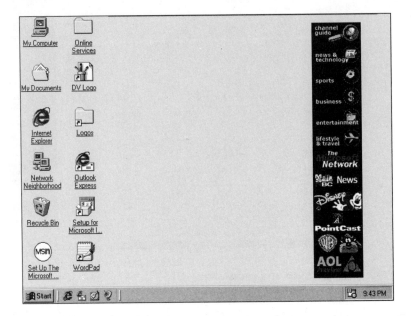

Remove shortcuts from your Desktop

In this exercise, you delete two shortcuts you no longer need.

1   Drag the DV Logo icon to the Recycle Bin.

A message asking if you are sure you want to send the DV Logo shortcut to the Recycle Bin is displayed.

②   Click the Yes button.

The DV Logo shortcut is removed from the Desktop and placed in the Recycle Bin.

③   Drag the Logos icon to the Recycle Bin.

A message asking if you are sure you want to send the Logos shortcut to the Recycle Bin is displayed.

④   Click the Yes button.

The Logos shortcut is removed from the Desktop and placed in the Recycle Bin.

Customize Desktop Colors and Backgrounds

Like placing a picture on your desk, you can tailor the computer workspace to fit your personality. For example, you can change the colors used for windows, buttons, and menus. You can also display any one of a variety of Desktop backgrounds as well as change the screen saver.

Each element of a window, such as the title bar or the border, is assigned a color. The combination of colors in a window is called a color scheme. Windows 98 includes color schemes designed specifically for certain types of monitors as well for people who need to work with large size print. There is also a wide range of color schemes to choose from.

Change your Desktop colors

 Right-click a blank area on the Desktop.

A shortcut menu is displayed.

 Click Properties.

The Display Properties dialog box appears.

 Click the Appearance tab.

The Appearance tab is active.

Sample display

 Click the Scheme down arrow, and then click Pumpkin (large).

The colors in the sample display change to the Pumpkin (large) color scheme. A large color scheme is one that uses larger print size, or font, on the title bar, buttons, and menus.

Larger
font

5 Click the Scheme down arrow, and then click Storm (VGA).

A VGA color scheme is one designed to work particularly well on a VGA monitor.

6 Click the Apply button.

The color scheme is applied to your Desktop.

Windows Standard is the default color scheme.

7 Continue sampling the color schemes until you find one you feel comfortable with.

8 Click the OK button.

The Display Properties dialog box closes, and the color scheme you chose is displayed.

Choose a Windows 98 background

In this exercise, you apply the Blue Rivets background.

1 Right-click a blank area on the Desktop.

A shortcut menu is displayed.

2 Click Properties.

The Display Properties dialog box appears, and the Background tab is active.

3 Scroll down the list of Wallpaper options, and then click Blue Rivets.

The wallpaper is displayed in the picture of the sample monitor.

Display Properties

Background | Screen Saver | Appearance | Effects | Web | Settings |

Sample of
wallpaper

Wallpaper
Select an HTML Document or a picture:

1stboot
Black Thatch
Blue Rivets
Bubbles
Carved Stone

Browse...
Pattern...

Display:
Center

Display
down arrow

OK   Cancel   Apply

❹ Click the Display down arrow, and then click Tile.

When you tile a background, the picture is repeated across the monitor.

❺ Click OK.

The Display Properties dialog box closes, and the wallpaper is displayed on your Desktop.

Choose a screen saver

A screen saver changes your monitor display to a moving design if you don't use the keyboard or mouse for a period of time. This serves to make your monitor more pleasing to look at as well as hiding whatever you are currently working on from casual observers. In this exercise, you select and customize a screen saver.

❶ Right-click a blank area on the Desktop.

A shortcut menu is displayed.

❷ Click Properties.

The Display Properties dialog box appears.

❸ Click the Screen Saver tab.

❹ Click the Screen Saver down arrow, and then click 3D Flower Box.

*Moving your
mouse while
a screen saver
is displayed
stops the
screen saver.*

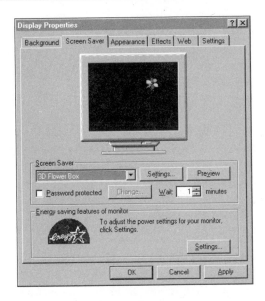

⑤   Click the Preview button.

The screen saver is turned on so that you can preview it.

⑥   Move your mouse or press any key to stop the screen saver preview.

⑦   Click the Settings button.

The 3D Flower Box Setup dialog box appears.

⑧   Click the Shape down arrow, and then click Spring.

⑨   Click OK.

The new shape is displayed in the screen.

New
shape

⑩ Continue sampling the other screen savers, and then select the screen saver you want to use.

⑪ In the Wait box, type the number of minutes that the computer should be inactive before the screen saver starts.

You can change this number if the time is too long or too short.

⑫ When you have chosen a screen saver, click OK.

The Display Properties dialog box closes, and the screen saver you have chosen will start when you stop using the keyboard or mouse for the amount of time you chose in the Wait box.

Set a screen saver password

One important use of a screen saver password is to protect your computer from being used by others while you are away from your desk. If you don't use your computer for a while, your screen saver will begin. You can set a password on the screen saver so that once the screen saver begins to run, you have to type the password to continue working. In this exercise, you set the screen saver password to the word "pass."

❶ Be sure that the Display Properties dialog box is displayed and the Screen Saver tab is active. Select the Password Protected check box, and then click the Change button.

The Change Password dialog box appears.

❷ In the New Password box, type **pass**

Asterisks appear as you type so that others do not see your password.

❸ Press TAB, and then in the Confirm New Password box, type **pass**

You type the password twice to ensure accuracy.

❹ Click OK.

A message informing you that the password has been successfully changed is displayed.

❺ Click OK again.

6 Click OK a third time to close the Display Properties dialog box.

Changes to the screen saver are saved. The next time the screen saver appears you will be prompted for a password to stop it.

One Step Further

Making Pictures into Backgrounds

One of the most popular ways to customize the Desktop is to create or scan a picture and then assign that picture as the Desktop background. For example, you can assign a scanned image of a friend or family member as the Desktop background. You first save the file in GIF format to a convenient location on your hard disk. If you have questions about saving an image you created or scanned, use the documentation that came with the art program or scanner.

You want to stay focused on a particular project for one of your clients so you decide to assign a client logo as your Desktop background.

Assign a picture to the Desktop background

In this exercise, you use My Computer to locate a graphic file and then apply it as a background.

1 Right-click a blank area on the Desktop.

A shortcut menu is displayed.

2 Click Properties.

The Display Properties dialog box appears, and the Background tab is active.

3 Click the Browse button.

The Browse dialog box appears.

4 Click the Up One Level button.

5 Double-click the Windows 98 SBS Practice folder.

The Windows 98 SBS Practice folder opens.

6 Double-click the Client Logos folder. The Client Logos folder opens.

7 Click the ProseWare Corporation icon, and then click the Open button.

The ProseWare Corporation logo is displayed.

8 Click the Display down arrow, and then click Stretch.

The logo is stretched to fill the entire Desktop.

9 Click OK.

The ProseWare Corporation logo is displayed on the Desktop.

Finish the lesson

1 To continue to the next lesson, drag any shortcuts you created to the Recycle Bin. Close any open windows.

2 If you are finished using your computer for now, click the Start button, and then click Shut Down.

The Shut Down Windows dialog box appears.

3 Select the Shut Down option, and click OK.

The Windows 98 logo appears as the computer shuts down.

Lesson 2 Quick Reference

To	Do this	Button
View the Desktop as a Web page	Right-click a blank area on the Desktop. Point to Active Desktop, and then click View As Web Page.	
Close the channel bar	Point to the top of the channel bar. Click the Close button on the gray bar.	
Display the channel bar	Right-click the Desktop. Point to Active Desktop, and then click Customize My Desktop. Select the Internet Explorer Channel Bar check box. Click OK.	
Apply the Web style to your Desktop and folders	Right-click the Desktop. Point to Active Desktop, and then click Customize My Desktop. Click Folder Options. Click Yes. Select the Web Style option, and click OK.	
Select and open icons and folders in Web Style display mode	Point to the icon or folder, and then click.	
View drive and folder information	Click the My Computer icon. Point to a drive. Point to a folder.	
View contents of drives and folders	Click the My Computer icon. Click a drive, and then click a folder icon.	
Display folder contents using the mouse and navigator buttons	Click the My Computer icon. Click a drive. Click a folder. Click another folder. Click the Back button. Click the Forward button. Click the Up One Level button.	
Display folder contents using the address bar	Type the location of the folder in the address bar, and press ENTER.	
Add new active content items to the Desktop	Right-click the Desktop. Point to Active Desktop, and then click Customize My Desktop. Click New. Select an item from the Active Desktop Gallery. Click OK.	
Move active content windows	Point to the top of the active content item window. Click and drag the title bar.	
Close active content windows	Point to the top of the active content item window, and then click the Close button.	☒
Create a shortcut to a program	Click the Start button, and point to Programs. Locate the program you want. Right-click the program, and then drag it to the Desktop. Click Create Shortcut(s) Here.	

Lesson 2 Quick Reference

To	Do this
Create a shortcut to a file or folder	Locate the file or folder in the My Computer window. Right-click and drag it to the Desktop. Click Create Shortcut(s) Here.
Remove a shortcut	Drag the shortcut icon to the Recycle Bin. Click Yes to confirm the deletion.
Arrange icons on the Desktop	Right-click a blank area on the Desktop. Point to Arrange Icons, and then click By Name.
Change the Desktop colors	Right-click a blank area on the Desktop. Click Properties. Click the Appearance tab. Click the Scheme down arrow, and then click a color scheme. Click OK.
Change the Desktop background	Right-click a blank area on the Desktop. Click Properties. Scroll through the list of backgrounds, and then click the background you want. Click OK.
Change screen savers	Right-click a blank area on the Desktop. Click Properties. Click the Screen Saver tab. Click the Screen Saver down arrow, and then click a screen saver. Click OK.
Set a screen saver password	Right-click a blank area on the Desktop. Click Properties. Click the Screen Saver tab. Click the Screen Saver down arrow, and then click a screen saver. Select the Password Protected check box, and then click the Change button. In the New Password box, type a password. In the Confirm New Password box, retype the password. Click OK. Click OK again.

3

Organizing Your Files and Folders

ESTIMATED TIME
40 min.

In this lesson you will learn how to:

- ✓ *Display files and folders in different ways.*
- ✓ *Create new folders to organize your files.*
- ✓ *Copy and move files and folders from one location to another.*
- ✓ *Search for files and programs using the Find File command.*
- ✓ *Delete and restore files.*

As your firm upgrades to Microsoft Windows 98, you decide to reevaluate how and where you store files on the computer. In the past you saved all your files in a single location. Now you want to organize your files in folders and to delete any unneeded files to save space on your hard disk.

Windows 98 offers tools to help you organize your computer files. In this lesson, you will learn how to display files and folders in the My Computer window. You will create folders and copy and move files to the new folders. You will also learn how to find files by name and file type. Finally, you will delete files and learn how to recover deleted files.

Viewing Information About Your Files and Folders

Generally folders and files are displayed in Windows 98 as large icons with the folder name or file name under the icon. This view makes it easy to see the file or folder, but it doesn't provide information about the size of the file, when it was created, or what program was used to create it. Also, depending on the size of the window and the number of files in the folder, all the files might not be visible in the window. There are other views available that offer additional detail or display a greater number of files. For example, the Details view reveals the file name, size, type, and last modification date and time. The List view displays only the file name, but arranges the files in columns so you can see more files. The Small Icons view displays only the file name, but arranges the files in rows.

Using different views can be very useful to you. Imagine you have 20 files for a particular client and your current view is Large Icons. Because not all the icons would fit in the window, you wouldn't see all 20 files at once and you might have to scroll to find a file. If you use the List view or the Small Icons view, you would be able to see all of your files for this client at once. You can have different views for each folder. For example, you can use the Large Icons view for your My Documents folder and use the Details view for your client folders. Each view in a folder is completely independent.

On your computer, you have a folder containing all the client logos you've worked on. You experiment with displaying the files in this folder using different views.

Change file display views

In this exercise, you view the contents of the Client Logo folder in the different views.

❶ Click the My Computer icon.

The My Computer window opens.

Maximize

❷ To view the entire contents of the My Computer window, click the Maximize button.

❸ Click the drive C icon, click the Windows 98 SBS Practice folder, and then click the Client Logos folder.

The contents of the Client Logos folder are displayed as large icons.

❹ On the Standard toolbar, click the down arrow to the right of the Views button, and then click Small Icons.

The contents are displayed as small icons and arranged in rows.

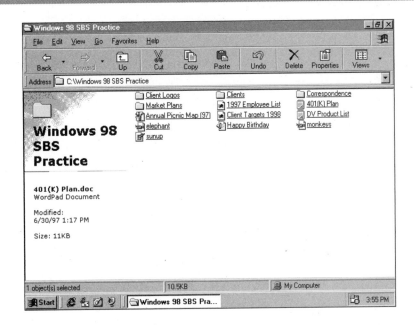

⑤   Click the down arrow to the right of the Views button, and then click List.

The contents are displayed in columns.

⑥   Click the down arrow to the right of the Views button, and then click Details.

The name, size, type, and last modification date of the contents are arranged in columns.

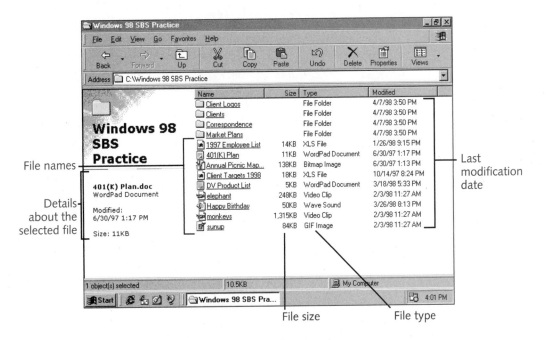

❼ Click the down arrow to the right of the Views button, and then click Large Icons.

❽ Close the My Computer window.

Sorting your files

By using the Arrange Icons command, you can sort your files by name, by size, by type, or by last modification date. The Arrange Icons command is available in any view. While you can use the Details view to see the file name, size, type, and last modification date, you can also use the column headings in this view to sort the files. For example, you have several logo files, marketing proposals, and budget spreadsheets in a single folder. You can sort the files by type so that all the logos are together, all the marketing proposals are together, and all the spreadsheets are together. When you create a file in a program and save it, it becomes a file type. You can tell what program was used to create the file by the icon associated with it. For example, when you create and save a file in Paint, the icon is represented by a pencil holder in front of a piece of paper with pencils and pens in the pencil holder.

You would like to find a client logo you created several months ago. You know the file was created in the Paint program, and you know approximately when you created it, but you cannot remember the name of the file.

Sort your files by modification date, size, and file name

In this exercise, you sort files first by their type, then by their last modification date, and lastly by name.

❶ Be sure that the Windows 98 SBS Practice folder is open. Click the Client Logos folder.

The Client Logos folder opens.

❷ Right-click a blank area on the Client Logos window, point to Arrange Icons, and then click By Type.

The files are arranged by type. Notice that the logos (created in the Paint program) are listed first, followed by the GIF image files.

When you sort a folder that contains both folders and files, the folders are listed first and then the files are listed.

❸ On the Standard toolbar, click the down arrow to the right of the Views button, and then click Details.

The view changes to show the details of the files.

❹ Click the Size heading at the top of the list of file details.

The files are sorted by size from smallest to largest.

⑤ Click the Modified column heading.

The files are sorted by last modification date from oldest to most recent.

⑥ Click the Name column heading.

The files are sorted alphabetically.

⑦ On the Standard toolbar, click the down arrow to the right of the Views button, and then click Large Icons.

The contents are displayed as large icons.

⑧ Close the Client Logos window.

Organizing Files Within Folders to Create Your Own Filing System

Every time you create a new marketing proposal or budget plan for a client, you need to save the file. When you save a file, the information is copied from the computer's temporary storage to permanent storage. You also need to choose the folder, or location, when you save a file. A folder is a container in which documents, program files, and other folders are stored on your computer. Folders allow you to separate materials by function or topic. For example, the Windows 98 installation program stores the files needed to run the computer in the Windows folder on your hard disk.

For a demonstration of how to create folders and subfolders, in the AVIFiles folder on the Microsoft Windows 98 Step by Step CD-ROM, double-click the page66 icon.

You can create folders to organize your work. Just as you might use folders in the drawers of a filing cabinet to store documents about your clients, you can create a computer filing system to store electronic files. Exactly how you design the filing system is up to you. If you share your computer in the home or office, a good place to start is with a folder for each of the users. Perhaps you work with several clients and would like to create a folder for each client. Alternatively, you can create folders for each type of work: letters, press releases, or balance sheets. You can use folders within a folder, known as subfolders, for even more accuracy. For example, within a client's folder you can create a marketing folder and a budget folder. It is also a good idea to store all your document folders in one location, such as the My Documents folder. This makes it easier to make back up copies of all your work at the same time or to search for files you have created. Just remember to be clear in how you name the folders and consistent in where you store the files.

Create new folders

You will use the Windows 98 SBS Practice folder for the following exercises to ensure that your practice folders are deleted when you delete the practice files for the book.

In this exercise, you create folders and subfolders in which you will store all the files for your new client.

1 Click the My Computer icon.

The My Computer window opens.

2 Click the drive C icon, and then click the Windows 98 SBS Practice folder.

The Windows 98 SBS Practice folder opens.

3 Right-click a blank area in the Windows 98 SBS Practice window.

A shortcut menu is displayed.

4 Point to New, and then click Folder.

A new folder appears in the Windows 98 SBS Practice window with the folder name, New Folder, highlighted. If you accidentally click the window or press ENTER, the folder will be named New Folder. You can go to the next exercise to rename the folder.

5 Type **Rogue** and press ENTER.

The folder is renamed to Rogue.

6 Click the new Rogue folder.

The Rogue folder opens. You will now create new subfolders within the Rogue folder.

7 Right-click a blank area in the Rogue window.

A shortcut menu is displayed.

8 Point to New, and then click Folder.

A new folder appears in the Rogue window with the folder name, New Folder, highlighted.

9 Type **Logos and Graphics** and press ENTER.

The Logos and Graphics subfolder within the Rogue folder appears. You will now create another new subfolder.

10 Right-click a blank area in the Rogue window.

A shortcut menu is displayed.

11 Point to New, and then click Folder.

A new folder appears in the Rogue window with the folder name, New Folder, highlighted.

12 Type **Marketing Plans** and press ENTER.

The folder is renamed.

Click the Up One Level button.

The Windows 98 SBS Practice folder opens.

Rename a folder

You realize you forgot to type the entire client name when you created the folder in the previous exercise. In this exercise, you change the name of the Rogue folder to Rogue Cellars.

1 Be sure that the Windows 98 SBS Practice folder is open. Right-click the Rogue folder.

A shortcut menu is displayed.

2 Click Rename.

The Rogue folder name is highlighted.

3 Type **Rogue Cellars** and press ENTER.

The folder is renamed to Rogue Cellars.

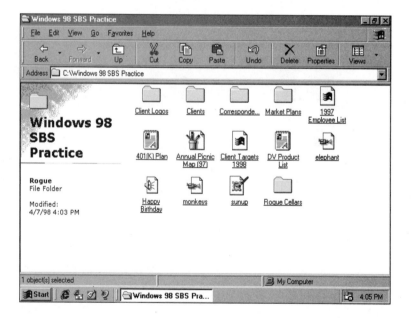

Copying and moving files and folders from one location to another

As your work needs change, you can copy or move files and folders from one location in your computer filing system to another. When you *copy* a file or folder, you duplicate the file or folder in a second location. For example, your new client, Rogue Cellars, has needs that are very similar to an existing client, Duffy Vineyards. You could save time in creating documents like a marketing plan or budget by copying files from the Duffy Vineyards folder to the Rogue Cellars folder. Once you have copied the files, you can edit the files so the information pertains to Rogue Cellars.

When you move a file or folder, the original is *cut*, or removed, from the first location and placed in the new location. You might use the Cut command if you reorganize your computer filing system and want to move files into different folders.

When you copy or cut a file or folder, a copy of the file or folder is temporarily stored in the *Clipboard*. The Clipboard is a temporary storage area. You then move to the new location and use the *paste* command to place a copy of the item there. A copy of the file or folder remains in the Clipboard until the next time you use the Copy or Cut command. This allows you to copy a file once, then paste copies of it to several other folders.

Sometimes, you need to copy or move more than one file from a single folder. There are two ways to copy and move multiple files at one time. If you are copying or moving adjacent files, you can click the first file, press and hold down the SHIFT key, and then click the last file that you want in the list. If you are copying or moving nonadjacent files, you can press and hold down the CTRL key while you click each file you need. When you choose the Cut or Copy command, all the selected files will be cut or copied.

You have set up a folder for Rogue Cellars, and you want to copy the marketing plan you used for Duffy Vineyards into the folder. You also created some logos for Rogue Cellars, but you saved them in the Client Logos folder and you want to move them to the Rogue Cellars folder.

Copy files to another folder

In this exercise, you copy files from the Duffy Vineyards folder and the Client Logos folder into the Rogue Cellars folder. First, you copy a single file and then you practice selecting and copying multiple files.

1   Be sure that the Windows 98 SBS Practice folder is open. Click the Market Plans folder.

2   Point to the Duffy Vineyards Plan file until the file detail information is displayed in the left pane.

  The name under the file is highlighted.

3   On the Standard toolbar, click the Copy button.

  The file is copied to the Clipboard.

4   In the Market Plans window, click the Up One Level button, click the Client Logos folder, and then click the Rogue Cellars Logos folder.

  The Rogue Cellars Logos folder opens.

5   On the Standard toolbar, click the Paste button.

  A copy of the Duffy Vineyards Plan file is placed in the Rogue Cellars Logos folder.

6   In the Rogue Cellars window, click the Up One Level button.

  The Client Logos folder opens.

7   To move all three Rogue Cellars logos, hold down the CTRL key, and click Rogue Cellars (Transparent). Keep holding down CTRL while you click Rogue Cellars Label and Rogue Cellars.

  All three files are highlighted.

8   On the Standard toolbar, click the Cut button.

  All three files are copied to the Clipboard.

9   In the Client Logos window, click the Rogue Cellars Logos folder.

  The Rogue Cellars Logos folder opens.

10   On the Standard toolbar, click the Paste button.

  The Rogue Cellars (Transparent), Rogue Cellars Label, and Rogue Cellars files are moved to the Rogue Cellars folder.

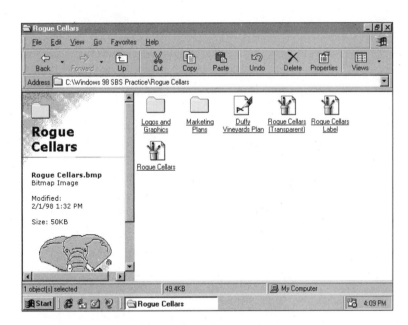

Move a file from one folder to another

In this exercise, you move the DV Product List file to the Rogue Cellars folder.

1 Be sure that the Windows 98 SBS Practice folder is open. Right-click DV Product List.

A shortcut menu is displayed.

2 Click Cut.

The DV Product List file is copied to the Clipboard. The file icon fades to indicate that it will be removed when you click the Paste button.

3 Click the Rogue Cellars folder.

The Rogue Cellars folder opens.

4 Right-click a blank area on the Rogue Cellars window.

A shortcut menu is displayed.

5 Click Paste.

The DV Product List file is placed in the Rogue Cellars folder. The original is removed from the Windows 98 SBS Practice folder.

6 In the Rogue Cellars window, click the Up One Level button.

Organizing Files and Folders

Move a folder

In this exercise, you move the Rogue Cellars folder to the Clients folder.

❶ Be sure that the Windows 98 SBS Practice folder is open. Point to the Rogue Cellars folder until it is highlighted.

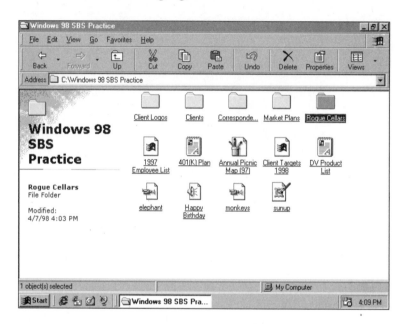

❷ On the Standard toolbar, click the Cut button.

The Rogue Cellars folder is copied to the Clipboard. The folder icon fades to indicate that it will be removed when you click the Paste button.

❸ In the Windows 98 SBS Practice window, click the Clients folder.

The Clients folder opens.

❹ On the Standard toolbar, click the Paste button.

The Rogue Cellars is placed in the Clients folder.

❺ Close the Clients window.

Searching for Files with Find File

Even with good file organization, sometimes you might forget the name or location of a file. If you can remember part of the name or what the file contained, the Find File command can help you locate the file on your hard disk or network.

You can use Find to search for files based on a variety of search criteria. You can search by file type, or limit the search to just a particular folder and subfolders. The broader your search criteria are the longer the search takes to finish. Therefore, any information you provide that narrows the search speeds the process. For example, if you can remember that the file was stored on your hard disk, as opposed to a network drive, then you can restrict your search to just the hard disk. Another way to narrow a search is to supply a date range, part of the file name, or the file type.

After you enter search criteria, you start the search by clicking the Find Now button. Find begins the search and opens a Results window displaying the files and folders meeting your criteria. You can open found files and folders directly from the Results window with a single click.

You created several files in the past few months. You can't remember the entire name of the files, but you do remember that one of the files contained the word "turkey" in the file name and the other contained the word "vineyard" in the file name. You also know you saved the files to your hard disk. You also need to find a letter you wrote to a landscaping agency regarding the caterpillar problem in the flower beds in front of the office. All you can remember is that the letter was about the caterpillars.

Find a file by partial file name

In this exercise, you use the Find File command to find files with "turkey" in the file name and then you look for files with "vineyard" in the file name. Finally, you open a found file from the Results window.

1 Click the Start button, point to Find, and then click Files Or Folders.

The Find dialog box appears.

Named box

Drive location

❷ In the Named box, type **turkey**

The search is limited to files that contain the word "turkey" in the file name.

❸ Click the Look In down arrow, and click drive C.

The search is limited to files on your hard disk.

❹ Click the Find Now button.

Find searches drive C for all files with "turkey" in the file name. When the search is complete, the files found appear in the Results window.

Results window

❺ To find the next file, click in the Named box, type **vineyard** and then click Find Now.

Find searches drive C for all files with "vineyard" in the file name. When the search is complete, the files found appear in the Results window.

❻ In the Results window, click Duffy Vineyards Plan.

The WordPad window opens and displays the Duffy Vineyards Plan file.

❼ Close the WordPad window.

Find a file by contents

In this exercise, you find a file by searching for a word contained in the file.

For a demonstration of how to find a document, in the AVIFiles folder on the Microsoft Windows 98 Step by Step CD-ROM, double-click the page75 icon.

①   Be sure that the Find window is open. Click the New Search button.

A message indicating that your current search will be cleared is displayed.

②   Click OK.

All the existing search criteria are cleared, allowing you to start entering criteria for a new search.

③   In the Containing Text box, type **caterpillar**

The search is limited to files that contain the word "caterpillar" somewhere within the file.

④   Click the Browse button.

The Browse For Folder dialog box appears. You can select a specific search location on your hard disk.

⑤   In the Browse For Folder dialog box, double-click drive C.

The list expands to show the contents of drive C.

⑥   Click the Windows 98 SBS Practice folder, and click OK.

The Look In box is filled in, and your search is limited to only the files in the Windows 98 SBS Practice folder and subfolders.

⑦   Click the Find Now button.

Find searches the Windows 98 SBS Practice folder for files that contain the text "caterpillar." The only file that contains the search word is a file named Garden.

Find a program

In this exercise, you use the Find command to find and then start the Paint program.

1 Be sure that the Find window is open. Click the New Search button.

A message indicating that your current search will be cleared is displayed.

2 Click OK.

All the existing search criteria are cleared, allowing you to start entering criteria for a new search.

3 In the Named box, type **paint**

The search is limited to files with the word "paint" in the file name.

4 Click the Look In down arrow, and click drive C.

The search is limited to files on your hard disk.

5 Click the Advanced tab.

Of Type down arrow

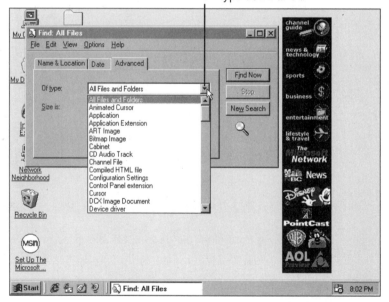

6 Click the Of Type down arrow, click Application, and then click the Find Now button.

By selecting Application in the Of Type box, the search is limited to program files. ("Application" is another term for "program.") When you click Find Now, drive C is searched and programs with the word "paint" in the file name are displayed in the Results window.

7 In the Results window, click Mspaint.

The Paint program starts.

8 Close the Paint window.

9 Close the Find window.

Deleting Files and Folders

Another facet of organization is cleanup. You still have files and folders for former clients. The old files and folders need to be deleted to conserve space on your hard disk. When a file or folder is deleted from the hard disk, it is actually moved to the Recycle Bin. The Recycle Bin is a folder that is used to temporarily store files and folders you deleted on your hard disk. Files deleted from a floppy disk or network are immediately removed and not stored in the Recycle Bin.

If you accidentally delete a file, you can restore it from the Recycle Bin. However, if you empty the Recycle Bin, the file is permanently deleted. It is important to empty the Recycle Bin periodically to ensure the maximum amount of available hard disk space.

Delete files

In this exercise, you delete an old 401(K) Plan file and Client Target list from the Windows 98 SBS Practice folder.

1 Click the My Computer icon.

The My Computer window opens.

2 Click the drive C icon, and then click Windows 98 SBS Practice.

The Windows 98 SBS Practice folder opens.

3 Right-click the 401(K) Plan file.

A shortcut menu is displayed.

❹ Click Delete.

A message asking you to confirm the deletion is displayed.

❺ Click the Yes button.

The 401(K) Plan file moves to the Recycle Bin.

❻ Point to the Client Targets 1998 file, and then press the DELETE key.

A message asking you to confirm the deletion is displayed.

❼ Click the Yes button.

The Client Targets 1994 file moves to the Recycle Bin.

Recover a deleted file from the Recycle Bin

In this exercise, you delete the Annual Picnic Map file and then use the Recycle Bin to restore the file.

❶ Be sure that the Windows 98 SBS Practice folder is open. Right-click the Annual Picnic Map (97) file.

A shortcut menu is displayed.

❷ Click Delete.

A message asking you to confirm the deletion is displayed.

❸ Click the Yes button.

The Annual Picnic Map (97) file moves to the Recycle Bin.

❹ To see the Recycle Bin icon, minimize the Windows 98 SBS Practice folder.

The Windows 98 SBS Practice folder is minimized to a button on the taskbar,
and the Desktop is displayed.

❺ On the Desktop, click the Recycle Bin icon.

The Recycle Bin window opens.

❻ Point to the Annual Picnic Map (97) file.

The Annual Picnic Map (97) file is selected, and its former location is displayed on the left side of the Recycle Bin window.

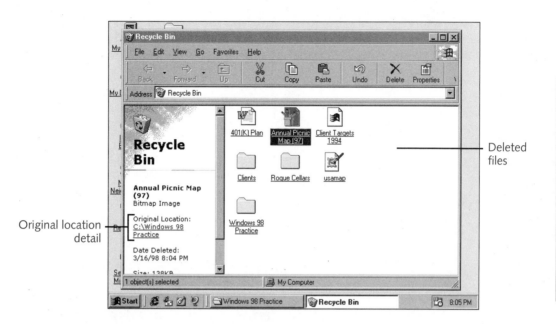

Deleted files

Original location detail

7 Right-click the Annual Picnic Map (97) file.

A shortcut menu is displayed.

8 Click Restore.

The Annual Picnic Map (97) file moves to its former location in the Windows 98 SBS Practice folder.

9 Close the Recycle Bin window.

10 On the taskbar, click the Windows 98 SBS Practice button.

The Windows 98 SBS Practice window opens. The Annual Picnic Map (97) file is restored to its former location.

11 Close the Windows 98 SBS Practice window.

Empty the Recycle Bin

In some corporate environments, options in Windows 98 have been set so that the Recycle Bin is automatically emptied when the computer is shut down.

In this exercise, you empty the Recycle Bin to permanently delete everything it contains.

① On the Desktop, right-click the Recycle Bin icon.

A shortcut menu is displayed.

② Click Empty Recycle Bin.

A message asking you to confirm the deletion is displayed. This is your last chance to change your mind before files are permanently deleted.

③ Click the Yes button.

The files are permanently removed from the Recycle Bin.

tip

While you can empty the Recycle Bin without actually opening it, you might want to see the files you are deleting before you empty the Recycle Bin. When you open the Recycle Bin window, you can use the Empty Recycle Bin command found on the File menu.

One Step Further Customizing Your Folders

 New!

One of the new features of Windows 98 is the ability to create a custom view of a folder by adding pictures to the background of a folder. You can customize just one folder or all your folders. You can also choose different pictures for each folder. If you find that you don't like the customized look you created for a folder, you can remove it.

Customize a folder

In this exercise, you use the Customize This Folder Wizard to change the background and color of the text of the Windows 98 SBS Practice folder.

① Click the My Computer icon, click the drive C icon, and then click the Window 98 Practice folder.

The Windows 98 SBS Practice folder opens.

② Right-click a blank area in the Windows 98 SBS Practice window.

A shortcut menu is displayed.

❸　Click Customize This Folder.

The Customize This Folder Wizard dialog box appears.

❹　Click Choose A Background Picture, and then click Next.

A list of backgrounds is displayed.

❺　Click the Circles.bmp file.

A sample of the Circles.bmp file is displayed in the left pane.

❻　In the Icon Caption Colors area, click the black box to the right of the text.

A color palette is displayed.

❼　Select white in the lower-right corner, and click OK.

The color white is selected, and the color palette closes.

❽　Click Next.

A message informing you that you are changing your background is displayed.

❾　Click Finish.

The background of your folder has changed, and the captions under the icons are white.

Remove folder customization

In this exercise, you remove the customization from the Windows 98 SBS Practice folder to make the contents and files in this folder easier to see.

❶　Click the My Computer icon, click the drive C icon, and then click the Windows 98 SBS Practice folder.

The contents of the Windows 98 SBS Practice folder are displayed.

❷　Right-click a blank area in the Windows 98 SBS Practice folder.

A shortcut menu is displayed.

❸　Click Customize This Folder.

The Customize This Folder Wizard dialog box appears.

❹　Click Remove Customization, and then click Next.

A message informing you that you are about to remove the folder's customization is displayed.

❺　Click Finish.

The customization is removed.

❻　Close the Windows 98 SBS Practice folder.

Finish the lesson

 To continue to the next lesson, close all open windows.

2 If you are finished using your computer for now, click the Start button, and then click Shut Down.

The Shut Down Windows dialog box appears.

3 Select the Shut Down option, and click OK.

The Windows 98 logo appears as the computer shuts down.

Lesson 3 Quick Reference

To	Do this
Display folder contents as large icons	Click the down arrow to the right of the Views button. Click Large Icons.
Display folder contents as small icons	Click the down arrow to the right of the Views button. Click Small Icons.
Display folder contents in a list	Click the down arrow to the right of the Views button. Click List.
Display details of folder contents	Click the down arrow to the right of the Views button. Click Details.
Sort folder contents by name, date, size, or file type	On the View menu, point to Arrange Icons, and then click one of the items in the list.
Create a new folder	Right-click a blank area in an open window. Point to New. Click Folder. Type the name of the folder. Press ENTER.
Rename a folder	Right-click the folder icon. Click Rename. Type the new name. Press ENTER.
Copy a file or folder from one location to another	Click the folder or file icon. On the Standard toolbar, click the Copy button. Click the destination. On the Standard toolbar, click the Paste button.

Lesson 3 Quick Reference

To	Do this
Move a file or folder from one location to another	Click the folder or file icon. On the Standard toolbar, click the Cut button. Click the destination. On the Standard toolbar, click the Paste button.
Select multiple files or folders	Hold down the CTRL key. Click the desired files and folders without releasing the CTRL key.
Search for a file or folder by partial file name or folder name	Click Start. Point to Find. Click Find Files Or Folders. In the Find window, type the partial name in the Named box. Click Find Now.
Search for a file by file type	Click Start. Point to Find. Click Find Files Or Folders. In the Find window, click the Advanced tab. Under Of Type, select the file type. Click Find Now.
Search for a file or folder by location	Click Start. Point to Find. Click Find Files Or Folders. In the Find window, click the Browse button. Select the location you want to search. Click OK.
Delete a file or folder	Click the file or folder icon. Click the Delete button. Click Yes. *or* Right-click the file or folder icon. Click Delete. Click Yes.
Restore a deleted file or folder	Click the Recycle Bin icon. Right-click the file or folder. Click Restore.
Empty the Recycle Bin	Right-click the Recycle Bin icon. Click Empty Recycle Bin. Click Yes. *or* Click the Recycle Bin icon. On the File menu, click Empty Recycle Bin, and then click Yes.

Organizing Files and Folders   3

LESSON

4

Modeling Windows 98 for Your Personal Use

ESTIMATED TIME
40 min.

In this lesson you will learn how to:

✔ *Reorganize Start menu commands.*

✔ *Add program shortcuts to the Start menu.*

✔ *Place shortcuts to frequently used items on the Favorites menu.*

✔ *Use online help to answer questions about Windows 98.*

Model Windows 98

Imagine your firm is well into the transition from the old and diverse computer system to Microsoft Windows 98. The more you explore Windows 98, the more evidence you find that the Desktop is a flexible and dynamic tool that encourages you to create the most efficient and comfortable working environment. You discover that one way to personalize the Desktop is to reorganize the commands on the Start menu. After spending some time exploring your customization options, you decide to use the online help files to learn more about Windows 98.

In this lesson, you will add and move Start menu commands. You will create shortcuts to frequently used files and folders and add them to the Favorites menu. To support your work with Windows 98, you will also learn how to search for help text on particular topics.

Customizing Your Desktop Menus

You might find that the shortcut to start the program you use most frequently is buried deep in cascading menus. For example, to start WordPad you must click Start, point to Programs, point to Accessories, and then click WordPad. By clicking a shortcut on a menu, you are giving your computer a command. To speed this process, you can drag a shortcut to a more convenient location on either the Start menu or the Desktop. In other words, you can move the WordPad shortcut from the bottom of the Accessories menu to the top of the Start menu. You can also drag the shortcut off the menu entirely to the Desktop.

Maybe you open a particular file or folder every day, such as a budget document or a list of potential clients. You can *right-drag* the file or folder to the Start menu and create a shortcut. To right-drag the file, you first click the file with the right mouse button. While holding down the right mouse button, you drag the file to a convenient location on the Start menu. When you release the right mouse button, a shortcut to the file appears on the menu.

You use WordPad every day to create documents for your clients. You notice that you have to go through several menus before you can open WordPad. You would like to be able to open WordPad quicker.

Move programs on your Start menu

For a demonstration of how to move programs to a more accessible place on the Start menu, in the AVIFiles folder on the Microsoft Windows 98 Step by Step CD-ROM, double-click the page86 icon.

In this exercise, you move the WordPad shortcut to a more accessible place on the Start menu. You then return it to its former location.

1 Click the Start button.

The Start menu is displayed.

2 On the Start menu, point to Programs, and then point to Accessories.

3 Position the mouse pointer on WordPad, press and hold down the left mouse button, and then drag WordPad to a blank area under the Windows Update command on the Start menu.

When you move the pointer, a gray box is displayed under the pointer. This is called a *ghost*. As you move the pointer on the Start menu, a black bar appears on the menu. This is called a *locator bar* and is used to show you where the object will be placed when you release the left mouse button.

Ghost

Black
locator
bar

❹   Release the left mouse button.

The WordPad shortcut is moved under Windows Update on the Start menu, and the Start menu closes.

❺   Click the Start button, point to Programs, and then point to Accessories.

WordPad is no longer displayed on the Accessories menu.

❻   To move WordPad back to the Accessories menu, point to WordPad on the Start menu, and then drag WordPad to Programs.

The Programs menu is displayed.

❼   On the Programs menu, point to Accessories, and then move the mouse pointer under the Paint program.

As you move down the Accessories menu, the locator bar appears.

❽   Release the left mouse button.

The WordPad shortcut moves from the Start menu to the Accessories menu.

❾   Click the Desktop.

The Start menu closes.

Move a program from the Programs menu to the Desktop

You use the Paint program to create logos. You would rather open it from the Desktop instead of from the Accessories menu. In this exercise, you move the Paint program from the Accessories menu to the Desktop.

1 Click the Start button.

The Start menu is displayed.

2 On the Start menu, point to Programs, and then point to Accessories.

3 Position the mouse pointer on Paint, press and hold down the left mouse button, and then drag the Paint shortcut to a blank area on the Desktop.

A shortcut of the Paint program appears on the Desktop.

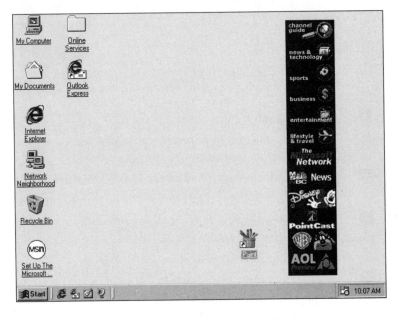

4 Click the Start button, point to Programs, and then point to Accessories.

The Paint shortcut is no longer displayed on the Accessories menu.

5 Click the Desktop.

The Start and Programs menus close.

Move an icon from the Desktop to the Accessories menu

You find that your Desktop has too many icons. You decide to move some of the icons to the Start menu. In this exercise, you move the Paint program to the Accessories menu.

❶ On the Desktop, right-click the Paint icon, and then drag Paint to the Start button.

A ghost of the Paint icon is displayed as you move the mouse pointer. When you point to the Start button, the Start menu is displayed.

❷ On the Start menu, point to Programs, and then point to Accessories.

As you move the pointer over Programs and Accessories, the black locator bar appears. The Accessories menu is displayed.

❸ Position the locator bar between Notepad and WordPad, and then release the right mouse button.

A shortcut menu is displayed.

❹ Click Move Here.

The shortcut menu closes, and the Paint object is displayed between Notepad and WordPad.

❺ Click a blank area on the Desktop.

The menus close, and the Paint object is no longer displayed on the Desktop.

Adding shortcuts to your Start menu

To make opening your files easier, you can add shortcuts to files you use frequently to your Start menu. By adding shortcuts to files to the Start menu, you can open the files without having to open My Computer and then open the folder in which they are located. For example, you have a client call list that you update every day. This file is located in a folder named Personal, which is located in the Employee folder. Every day, you click My Computer, drive C, Employee folder, and then Personal. You could open the file quicker if it were a shortcut located on the Start menu.

Add a file to your Start menu

In this exercise, you create a shortcut for a file located in the Windows 98 SBS Practice folder and place it on the Start menu.

❶ Click the My Computer icon.

The My Computer window opens.

❷ Click the drive C icon, and then click the Windows 98 SBS Practice folder.

The Windows 98 SBS Practice folder opens.

❸ With the left mouse button, drag 1997 Employee List to the Start button.

A ghost of the 1997 Employee List icon is displayed. The Start menu is displayed.

④ Point to the area below the Windows Update command.

The locator bar is displayed.

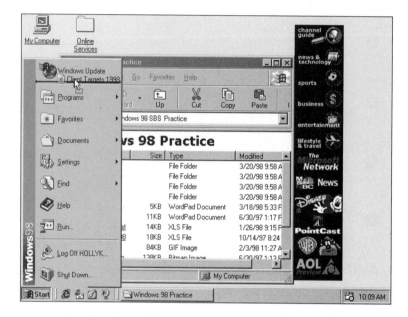

⑤ Release the left mouse button.

Since you only made a shortcut for your file, Shortcut to 1997 Employee List is displayed below the Windows Update shortcut.

⑥ Click the Desktop.

The Start menu closes.

⑦ Close the Windows 98 SBS Practice window.

Renaming shortcuts located on the Start menu

You can rename any of the shortcuts at the top of the Start menu or in the Programs menu. For example, when you create a shortcut on the Start menu, the words "Shortcut to" appear before the menu's name. To rename the shortcut, you use the Taskbar & Start Menu command found in the Settings menu on the Start menu.

You have moved your 1997 Employee List shortcut to the Start menu. When you moved it, you noticed that the words "Shortcut to" were added to the menu name.

Rename a shortcut on the Start menu

In this exercise, you use the Taskbar & Start Menu command to rename the shortcut.

1 Click the Start button.

The Start menu is displayed.

2 On the Start menu, point to Settings, and then click Taskbar & Start Menu.

The Taskbar Properties dialog box appears.

3 Click the Start Menu Programs tab.

4 Click the Advanced button.

The Exploring–Start Menu window opens. The Start menu is selected in the left pane, and the Shortcut to Client Targets icon, which is located on the Start menu, is displayed in the right pane.

5 Right-click Shortcut to 1997 Employee List.

A shortcut menu is displayed.

6 Click Rename.

A box appears around the object name, and the text is highlighted.

7 Type **1997 Employee List** and press ENTER.

The object is renamed.

8 Close the Exploring–Start Menu window.

Modeling Windows 98 for You   4

9 On the Taskbar Properties dialog box, click OK.

The dialog box closes.

Remove a command from the Start menu

In this exercise, you add a command to the Start menu. You will then remove the command.

1 Drag the Online Services icon on the Desktop to the Start button.

The Start menu is displayed.

2 Drop Online Services above the Programs command.

The shortcut to Online Services is displayed above the Programs command.

3 Click the Desktop.

The Start menu closes.

4 Click the Start button.

5 On the Start menu, right-click the shortcut to Online Services.

A shortcut menu is displayed.

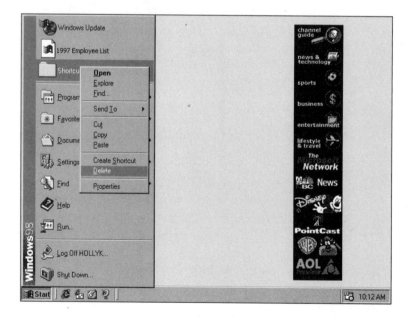

6 Click Delete.

A message asking you to confirm the deletion is displayed.

7 Click Yes.

The shortcut to Online Services moves to the Recycle Bin.

Starting Programs Automatically

Perhaps first thing every morning at your office, you check your electronic mail. It would be convenient if the electronic mail program Outlook Express started automatically. To make a program start or a file open as soon as Windows 98 starts, you add a shortcut of that program or file to the StartUp menu. The StartUp menu is included within the Start menu. Any shortcuts on the StartUp menu will automatically open when the computer starts. If you change your mind, you can drag the shortcut off the StartUp menu and move it into the Recycle Bin.

Add a shortcut to your StartUp folder

In this exercise, you add a shortcut to Outlook Express to the StartUp folder.

❶　Drag the Outlook Express shortcut on the Desktop to the Start button but do not release the left mouse button.

The Start menu is displayed.

❷　Continue to hold down the left mouse button, and then point to Programs.

❸　Continue to hold down the left mouse button, point to the StartUp menu, when the menu opens, release the button.

❹　Point to the StartUp menu to see the new shortcut.

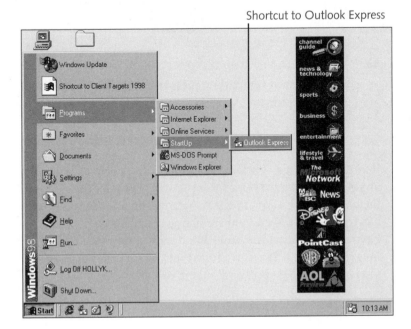

Shortcut to Outlook Express

5   Click the Desktop to close the Start menu.

Restart Windows 98 to test your new StartUp shortcut

In this exercise, you restart your computer to see Outlook Express start when Windows 98 starts.

1   Click the Start button.

2   On the Start menu, click Shut Down.

       The Shut Down Windows dialog box appears.

3   Select the Restart option, and click OK.

Close

       Windows 98 shuts down and then restarts. Outlook Express starts after Windows 98 starts. If the Welcome to Windows 98 window opens, click the Close button.

4   On the Outlook Express title bar, click the Close button.

Remove a shortcut from your StartUp folder

When your needs change, you might find that shortcuts you have added to the StartUp menu are no longer useful and slow the starting of your computer. In this exercise, you delete the Outlook Express shortcut you added to the StartUp menu in a previous exercise.

1   Click the Start button, point to Programs, and then point to StartUp.

2   On the StartUp menu, right-click Outlook Express.

       A shortcut menu is displayed.

3   Click Delete, and then click Yes.

       The Outlook Express shortcut is removed from the StartUp folder and placed in the Recycle Bin.

Creating and Using Favorites

For more information on displaying a Web page and adding it to the Favorites menu, see Lesson 5, "Understanding Networks, the Internet, and E-mail."

If you add too many shortcuts to the Start menu, it begins to look cluttered. Just as you can organize your files into multiple folders and subfolders, you can group the commands by type in the Programs and Favorites menus. The Programs menu has traditionally been used for listing shortcuts to your software applications. The Favorites menu, on the other hand, is a good place to list shortcuts to working files and folders. There are four types of objects you can add to the Favorites menu: file, folder, cascading menu, and Web page.

Add a document to the Favorites menu using the mouse

In this exercise, you place a shortcut to a document on the Favorites menu. You will then open the document from the menu.

❶ Click the My Computer icon, click the drive C icon, and then click the Windows 98 SBS Practice folder.

The Windows 98 SBS Practice folder opens.

❷ Click the Market Plan folder.

The Market Plan folder opens.

❸ Drag the MightyFlighty Plan file to the Start button.

The Start menu is displayed.

❹ On the Start menu, point to Favorites, and then drop the MightyFlighty Plan file at the top of the Favorites menu.

A shortcut to MightyFlighty Plan is displayed at the top of the Favorites menu.

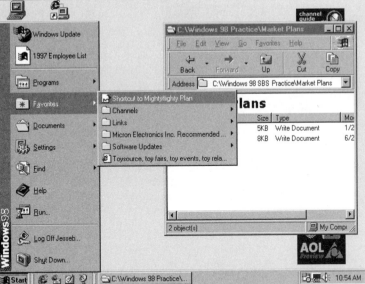

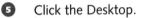

Close

If you have installed Microsoft Word, the Word program starts when you click a word processing document, such as MightyFlighty Plan.

❺ Click the Desktop.

❻ Close the My Computer window.

❼ On the Start menu, point to Favorites, and then click Shortcut to MightyFlighty Plan.

The WordPad program starts, and the MightyFlighty Plan file opens.

❽ Close the WordPad window.

Add a folder to the Favorites menu

In this exercise, you place a shortcut to a folder on the Favorites menu. You then open a new window displaying the folder contents from the menu command.

❶ Click the My Computer icon, and then click the drive C icon.

The Drive C window opens.

❷ Click the Windows 98 SBS Practice folder.

The Windows 98 SBS Practice folder opens.

❸ Click the Client Logos folder.

The Client Logos folder opens.

❹ On the Client Logos window menu bar, click Favorites.

The Favorites menu is displayed.

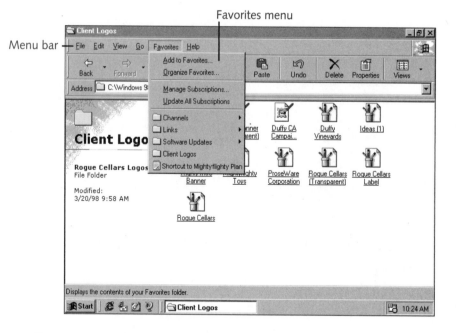

Favorites menu

Menu bar

❺ Click Add To Favorites.

The Add Favorite dialog box appears.

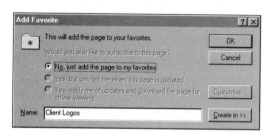

6 Click OK.

7 Close the My Computer window.

8 Click the Start button, point to Favorites, and then click Client Logos.

The Client Logos window opens.

9 Click the Minimize button.

Create a cascading menu on the Favorites menu

In this exercise, you create a menu on the Favorites menu and then you move a shortcut from the Favorites menu to the newly created menu.

1 Click the My Computer icon, and then click the drive C icon.

The Drive C window opens.

2 Click the Windows 98 SBS Practice folder, and then click the Client Logos folder.

The Client Logos folder opens.

3 On the Favorites menu, click Organize Favorites.

The Organize Favorites dialog box appears.

Modeling Windows 98 for You   4

*Create New
Folder*

④ Click the Create New Folder button.

A new folder appears at the end of the list of Favorites.

⑤ Type **Southwest Campaign** and press ENTER.

⑥ Close the Organize Favorites dialog box.

⑦ Drag the Duffy CA Banner file to the Start button.

The Start menu is displayed.

⑧ Point to Favorites, point to Southwest Campaign, and then drop the Duffy CA Banner file on the Southwest Campaign (Empty) menu.

The Southwest Campaign cascading menu appears with the disabled command (Empty). When you drop the Duffy CA Banner, it appears on the Southwest Campaign menu replacing (Empty).

⑨ Click the Desktop.

The Start, Favorites, and Southwest Campaign menus close.

⑩ Close the Client Logos window.

Getting Help with Windows 98

While a co-worker, friend, or family member might be able answer your questions about Windows 98, a more convenient source of advice is at your fingertips in the form of online help. Online help gives you instruction on using Windows 98. The help files include text on new Windows 98 features, Desktop objects and view modes, Windows 98 accessories, and a wide range of other topics.

In fact, the contents of the help files are so extensive that you have three ways of looking for help. You can search for a topic using the Index tab, the Search tab, or the Contents tab. The Index functions like an index at the back of a book. You type a word into the Index box, and the list scrolls through possible keywords as you type. When you identify a potentially useful keyword, you can click it to view the information. If there is only one topic using that keyword, the information appears to the right in the display pane. However, if there are multiple topics, you are provided with an opportunity to choose among them and then display the chosen topic in the display pane.

The Search feature is another tool to find particular help text. You can use the Search tab to find information about a broad topic. For example, if you want to find information about copying, but you don't want to limit it to just files and folders, you would use the Search tab. You supply a word or phrase and then the topics that contain that text are listed. You double-click a topic to display the help file text.

The Contents feature is organized like a table of contents. The Contents tab displays "chapters," which are represented with a book icon. When you click the icon, it expands to display topics or more chapters. Topics are represented by a page icon. The Contents tab also provides Tips and Tricks sections that can help you use Windows 98 more efficiently.

Find help using the Contents tab

In this exercise, you use the Contents tab to find information about the Active Desktop.

1   Click the Start button, and then click Help.

The Windows Help window opens.

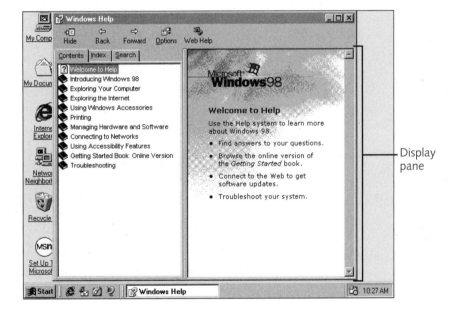

Display pane

Maximize

2   Click the Contents tab, and then click the Maximize button.

3   Point to Exploring Your Computer.

The pointer changes to a hand and highlights Exploring Your Computer.

4   Click Exploring Your Computer.

The menu expands to display topics under Exploring Your Computer.

5   Click The Windows Desktop, and then click Making the New Desktop Your Own.

The menu expands to display a list of topics under "Making the New Desktop Your Own."

6 Click "What is the Active Desktop."

Help text on "What is the Active Desktop" appears in the display pane to the right.

7 In the right display pane, scroll down to the Related Topics area, and then click "Turn on the Active Desktop interface."

The display pane text now displays steps on how to turn on the Active Desktop.

8 In the left display pane, click "Exploring Your Computer."

The menu collapses to conceal the subheadings under the "Exploring My Computer" topic. The display pane continues to display the steps on how to turn on the Active Desktop.

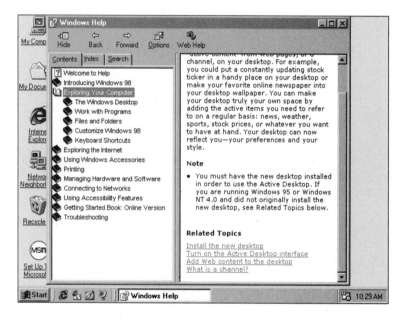

9 Close the Windows Help window.

Use the index to find help on a specific topic

In this exercise, you use the Index tab to locate steps for adding submenus to the Start menu.

1 Click the Start button, and then click Help.

The Windows Help window opens.

Maximize

2 Click the Index tab, and then click the Maximize button.

❸ In the Index box, type **start**

As you start to type, the list moves to topics that start with the letter "s" and then moves to words that start with "st" and so on.

❹ Under the Start menu subheading, click "adding submenus."

The phrase "Start menu, adding submenus" appears in the Index box.

❺ Click the Display button.

The display pane text changes to instructions on how to add a submenu to the Programs menu.

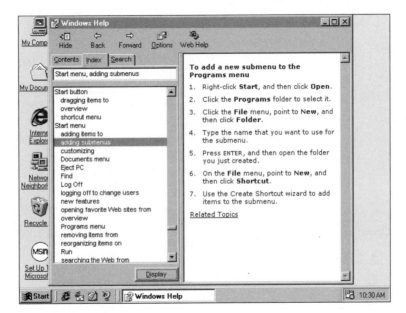

❻ In the keyword list, under the Start menu subheading, double-click "new features."

The display pane text changes to information about new Start menu features.

❼ Click the Back button.

The display pane text returns to instructions on how to add submenus to the Programs menu.

❽ Close the Windows Help window.

Find help on specific topics using the Search feature

In this exercise, you use the Search tab to identify and display topics containing the word "favorites."

1 Click the Start button, and then click Help.

The Windows Help window opens.

2 Click the Search tab, and then click the Maximize button.

3 In the Type In The Keyword To Find box, type **favorites**.

4 Click the List Topics button.

Topics with the word "favorites" appear in the Topics list.

Keyword box

Topic list

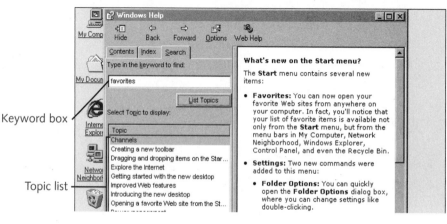

5 In the Topics list, click "What's new on the Start menu."

6 Click the Display button.

The display pane text changes to information about new items on the Start menu.

7 In the Topics list, double-click "Getting started with the new desktop."

The display pane text changes to information about getting started with the new Desktop.

8 Close the Windows Help window.

One Step Further

Adding Programs to the Taskbar

New!

The taskbar includes a Quick Launch toolbar with buttons to start programs. When you install Windows 98, four buttons appear: Show Desktop, Launch Outlook Express, Launch Internet Explorer Browser, and View Channels. You can add a button for a program you use frequently to the taskbar. For example, you want to quickly open a program that is located on the Programs menu but you don't want to create a shortcut on your Desktop. You can create a button on the taskbar so that you can quickly open the program without having to open the Start menu and then the Programs menu.

You use WordPad every day and you want to be able to open it quickly. You can't create a shortcut on your Desktop because you have many shortcuts and it is beginning to look cluttered.

Add WordPad to the taskbar

In this exercise, you create a button for WordPad on the taskbar by dragging the WordPad command to the taskbar.

1   Click the Start button.

The Start menu is displayed.

2   On the Start menu, point to Programs, point to Accessories, and then point to WordPad.

3   Right-drag WordPad to the Quick Launch toolbar on the taskbar.

A locator bar appears on the Quick Launch toolbar.

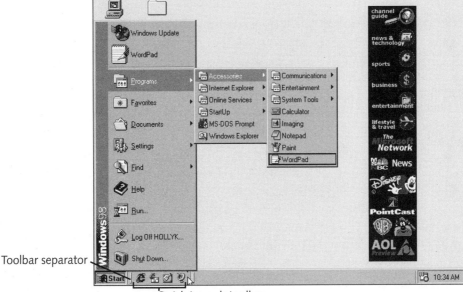

Toolbar separator

Quick Launch toolbar

④ Release the right mouse button.

A shortcut menu is displayed.

⑤ Click Create Shortcut(s) Here.

The WordPad button appears on the Quick Launch toolbar.

⑥ Drag the toolbar separator to the right a half inch.

The space allotted to the Quick Launch toolbar expands.

Remove a program icon from the taskbar

In this exercise, you remove the WordPad program from the taskbar.

① On the taskbar, right-click the WordPad button.

A shortcut menu is displayed.

② Click Delete.

A message asking you to confirm the deletion is displayed.

③ Click Yes.

WordPad is removed from the Quick Launch toolbar and moved to the Recycle Bin.

Finish the lesson

① To continue to the next lesson, close any open windows.

② Delete the 1997 Employee List file and the Online Services icon you added to the Start menu during the lesson. Right-click the command, and then click Delete. Click Yes.

③ Delete the MightyFlighty Plan file and the Client Logos folder you added to the Favorites menu during the lesson. Right-click the command, and then click Delete. Click Yes.

④ Return WordPad and Paint to their original location on the Accessories menus. Drag each program from its new location to its former location.

⑤ Delete the WordPad program icon you added during the lesson from the taskbar. Right-click the WordPad program icon, and then click Delete. Click Yes.

⑥ If you are finished using your computer for now, click the Start button, and then click Shut Down.

The Shut Down Windows dialog box appears.

⑦ Select the Shut Down option, and click OK.

The Windows 98 logo appears as the computer shuts down.

Lesson 4 Quick Reference

To	Do this
Move commands on your menus	Click the Start button. Point to Programs, and then point to a submenu. Drag the program you want to move to the desired location. Release the mouse button.
Move a command from the Start menu to the Desktop	Click the Start button. Point to the command you want to move to your Desktop. Drag the command to the Desktop, and release the mouse button.
Move a file or folder from the Desktop to the Start menu	Right-drag the file or folder to the Start button. Point to Programs, and then point to the menu where you want the file or folder to be located. Release the mouse button. On the shortcut menu, click Move Here.
Add a file or folder to the Start menu	Click the My Computer icon, and then click the drive C icon. Drag the file or folder you want on the Start menu to the Start button, and then drop it on its new location on the Start menu.
Rename commands on the Start menu	Click the Start button. Point to Settings, and then click Taskbar & Start Menu. Click the Start Menu Programs tab. Click the Advanced button. Right-click the command to be renamed, and then click Rename. Type the new name, and press ENTER.
Remove a program from the Start menu	Right-click the program. Click Delete. Click Yes.
Add a program to the StartUp menu	Drag the program to the Start button. Point to Programs, and then point to StartUp. Release the mouse button.

Modeling Windows 98 for You   4

Lesson 4 Quick Reference

To	Do this	Button
Remove a program from the StartUp menu	Click the Start button. Point to Programs, and then point to StartUp. Right-click the program, and click Delete.	
Add a file to the Favorites menu	Click the My Computer icon, and then click the drive C icon. Drag the file you want to add to Favorites to the Start button, and then drop it on the Favorites menu.	
Add a folder to the Favorites menu	Click the My Computer icon. Click the folder to be added to Favorites. On the Favorites menu, click Add To Favorites. Click OK.	
Add a menu to the Favorites menu	Click the My Computer icon. On the Favorites menu, click Organize Favorites. Click the Create New Folder button. Type the name of the menu, and press ENTER.	
Find help using the Contents tab	Click the Start button, and then click Help. Click the Contents tab. Click the topic you want.	
Find help using the Index tab	Click the Start button, and then click Help. Click the Index tab. Type a keyword, and then double-click the topic you want.	
Find help using the Search tab	Click the Start button, and then click Help. Click the Search tab. Type a word or phrase. Click List Topics. Double-click the topic you want.	
Add a program to the taskbar	Right-drag the program from the Programs menu to the Quick Launch toolbar. Click Create Shortcut(s) Here.	
Expand the portion of the taskbar allocated to programs	Drag the resizing border on the taskbar to the right.	
Remove a program from the taskbar	Right-click the program. Click Delete. Click Yes.	

Review & Practice

You will review and practice how to:

✔ *Open, close, and switch between programs.*

✔ *Control windows, programs, and icons on the Desktop.*

✔ *Organize the files and folders on your hard disk.*

✔ *Use online help to answer questions about using Windows 98.*

✔ *Enhance your Desktop with active content items that display regularly updated news and information.*

✔ *Customize your Desktop and add shortcuts to the Start and Favorites menus.*

ESTIMATED TIME 20 min.

Review & Practice

Before you move on to Part 2, which covers working with networks, the Internet, and electronic mail, you can practice the skills you learned in Part 1 by working through this Review & Practice section. You will review Windows 98 fundamentals; create folders; copy, move, and delete files; customize your Desktop; and add shortcuts to the Start and Favorites menus.

Scenario

Because you have made such progress in learning how to work with and customize the Microsoft Windows 98 Desktop, you are asked to help train a new partner who is unfamiliar with computers. You begin by reviewing the basics of how to use a mouse and display information about folders and files using the My Computer window. You assist with setting up a folder for your partner's principal client as well as demonstrate how to move, copy, and delete files. Then you introduce your partner to adding shortcuts to the menus and active content items to the Desktop. You also customize the Desktop with a new color scheme and background as well as present how to use online help to answer questions about Windows 98.

Step 1:   Work with Windows and Icons on the Desktop

You demonstrate to your partner the fundamentals of working with a mouse and Windows 98 first by moving icons on the Desktop and opening the My Computer window. You show how to open folders and display additional information about their contents. Finally, you use the Arrange Icons command as an example of how to display and use shortcut menus.

❶ Use the mouse to arrange Desktop icons alphabetically along the right side of the monitor.

❷ Open the My Computer window, and then open the Drive C window.

❸ Display the contents of the Market Plans folder located in the Windows 98 SBS Practice folder.

❹ Display the file details of the Market Plans folder, and then sort the files by size.

❺ Minimize the My Computer window.

❻ Use the Desktop shortcut menu to arrange the icons on your Desktop by size.

For more information about	See
Using the mouse to arrange Desktop objects	Lesson 1
Opening a Desktop icon	Lesson 1
Displaying folder contents and file information	Lesson 3
Minimizing a window	Lesson 1
Using a shortcut menu	Lesson 1

Step 2:   Open, Close, and Switch Between Programs

After explaining to your partner how Windows 98 lets you have more than one program open at the same time, you demonstrate opening, closing, and switching between programs with Calculator and Outlook Express.

 Use the Start menu to start the Calculator program.

❷   Use the button on the taskbar to start Outlook Express.

❸   Switch to Calculator.

❹   Close the Calculator and Outlook Express windows.

For more information about	See
Starting a program	Lesson 1
Switching between programs	Lesson 1
Closing programs	Lesson 1

Step 3:   Organize Your Files into Folders and Subfolders

Your partner wants to immediately start work for a client called MightyFlighty Toys. You help by creating a folder for the client in the Windows 98 SBS Practice folder. You then find, copy, and move files relating to the MightyFlighty Toys account into the new folder. Finally, you identify a few files that your partner won't need and delete them.

❶   Open the Market Plans window, and then create a new folder in the Windows 98 SBS Practice folder called Flighty.

❷   Rename the Flighty folder to MightyFlighty Toys.

❸   Find files on your computer with the word "mighty" in the file name.

❹   Copy the Mighty Intro Banner file from the Client Logos folder into the MightyFlighty Toys folder.

❺   Move the MightyFlighty Plan from the Market Plans folder to the MightyFlighty Toys folder.

❻   Delete the Get MightyFlighty Strategy and MightyFlighty Intro files from the Windows 98 SBS Practice folder.

❼   Recover the Get MightyFlighty Strategy file from the Recycle Bin, and then empty the Recycle Bin.

For more information about	See
Creating a new folder	Lesson 3
Renaming a file or folder	Lesson 3
Finding a file or folder	Lesson 3
Copying and moving a file or folder	Lesson 3
Deleting and recovering a file or folder	Lesson 3

Step 4:   Get Assistance with Windows 98

Since your partner will initially have many questions about how to use
Windows 98, you illustrate how to open and use the online help program.
You take the opportunity to learn more about adding an active content item,
such as a stock ticker, to the Desktop.

  Use the online help index to learn more about adding active content items
to the Desktop.

❷ Use the online search function to find help topics that discuss adding a
stock ticker to your Desktop. Hint: Search for the word "ticker."

For more information about	See
Finding online help using the index	Lesson 4
Finding online help using the search function	Lesson 4

Step 5:   Add Active Content Items to Your Desktop

Your partner is intrigued by the idea of adding a stock ticker to the Desktop.
You connect to the Active Desktop Gallery and add the Microsoft Investment
Ticker. You then resize the active content item and move it to a more convenient
place on the Desktop.

  Add the Microsoft Investment Ticker active content item to the Desktop.

❷ Make the stock ticker item one inch by four inches, and then move it to the
lower-right section of your monitor.

❸ Close the stock ticker item.

For more information about	See
Adding active content items to the Desktop	Lesson 2
Moving and sizing active item windows	Lesson 2
Closing active item windows	Lesson 2

**Step 6:   Personalize Your Desktop
with Colors, Backgrounds, and Shortcuts**

Working with your partner, you discover that he has trouble seeing some of the text on the monitor and would prefer soft colors with large print. You change the Desktop color scheme and also modify the screen saver and background. Finally, you show how shortcuts on the Desktop as well as the Start and Favorites menu can make working with files and programs quicker and more efficient.

1. Change the Desktop color scheme to Rose (large), the screen saver to 3D Maze with a 15-minute wait, and the background to tiled Bubbles.
2. Create a shortcut on the Desktop to the MightyFlighty Toys folder.
3. Move the Paint program from the Accessories menu to the Start menu.
4. Add the MightyFlighty Plan file to the Favorites menu.

For more information about	See
Customizing the Desktop color scheme, background, and screen saver	Lesson 2
Creating a shortcut to a file or folder on the Desktop	Lesson 2
Moving a menu command	Lesson 4
Adding a file to the Favorites menu	Lesson 4

Finish the Review & Practice

1. To continue to the next lesson, close all open windows and programs.
2. Change the color scheme, background, and screen saver to suit your personal preferences.
3. Remove shortcuts from the Desktop, Favorites menu, and Start menu that were created during the exercises.
4. If you are finished using your computer for now, click the Start button, and then click Shut Down.
5. Select the Shut Down option, and click OK.
   The Windows 98 logo appears as the computer shuts down.

PART 2

Working with Networks and the Internet

LESSON

5

Understanding Networks, the Internet, and E-mail

ESTIMATED TIME
40 min.

In this lesson you will learn how to:

✔ *Connect to and explore the World Wide Web.*

✔ *Find a Web site using search programs.*

✔ *Add a Web page to your Favorites menu.*

✔ *Subscribe to a Web page and receive notification when new information appears on the page.*

✔ *Exchange electronic mail messages with friends and co-workers.*

Imagine your public relations firm has 10 employees. There is only one laser printer and one scanner to meet everyone's needs. To allow everyone to use this equipment, the computers, printer, and scanner need to be connected. This connection of equipment is called a *network*. With a network, you and your co-workers can also share files, share software programs, and send one another e-mail. You can connect to many other organizations and individuals through the Internet. The Internet is a worldwide network of computers that people use to communicate with each other and exchange information.

In this lesson, you will learn about networks. You will connect to the Internet and use a Web browser to explore the World Wide Web. When you find a useful Web page, you will add the page to the Favorites menu so that you can easily connect to it again. With Microsoft Outlook Express, which is part of Windows 98, you will send and receive electronic mail messages.

Learning about Networks

A network is a group of computers that are connected by cables. Each work-station runs a special networking program so the computers can pass information back and forth. If your computer is part of a network, you connect, or log on, to the network using your username and password. The file server software checks your user ID and password to see if you have the right to use the network resources. Once you are logged on to the network, you can store your files on the network, share your files with co-workers, use network programs and resources such as printers, fax modems, and backup drives, or e-mail your co-workers. If your network is Internet capable, then you can send e-mail to your clients or search the Internet for information.

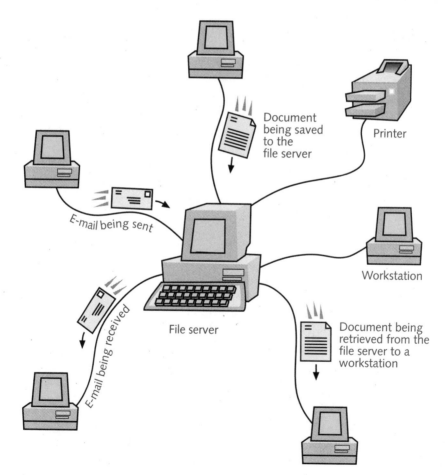

Even if you are connected to a network at work, you might not be able to con-nect to the Internet via your network. To connect to the Internet through your network, an Internet connection program must be installed on the computer that controls the network. If you are at home and not connected to a network, you can still connect to the Internet by using an Internet Service Provider. See Lesson 10, "Using Your Computer at Home," for more information about Internet Service Providers.

important

The following section assumes that you connect to the Internet through either a corporate network or a dial-up connection. For more information about establishing a dial-up connection, see Lesson 10, "Using Your Computer at Home."

Connecting to the World Wide Web

As part of a public relations firm, you require constant access to breaking news stories, market conditions, and ongoing research. For example, you might have a client whose business will be dramatically affected by the passing of a law, and so you need to monitor national news services. The World Wide Web offers the quickest and most cost-effective way to gather this information.

All over the world, organizations and individuals create *Web sites*. A Web site is collection of *Web pages* available at one location. A Web page is a file that contains text, pictures, or both. A Web page can also contain *links*. Links are text or graphics you click to move to a new Web page or to a different location on the same Web page. The World Wide Web is the collection of all Web sites available on the Internet.

Viewing Web pages with your browser window

Part of your services to your clients is performing research. For example, you might research a competitor's new product or you might find information to help clients expand their business. One of the tools you want to use for your research is the Web. To perform your research, you open your browser window. When the browser window opens, your default *home page* is loaded. A home page is the Web page your browser connects to every time you start your Web browser. From your home page, you can go to additional pages by clicking links or by typing the Web page address of a particular Web page directly into the address bar.

Open the browser window

You only need to do step 1 of this exercise if you have an Internet connection through your corporate network. The remaining steps are for a dial-up connection.

Launch Internet Explorer Browser

1   On the taskbar, click the Launch Internet Explorer Browser button.

The browser window opens. If you are using a dial-up connection and are not currently connected to your Internet Service Provider (ISP), the Dial-Up Connection dialog box appears.

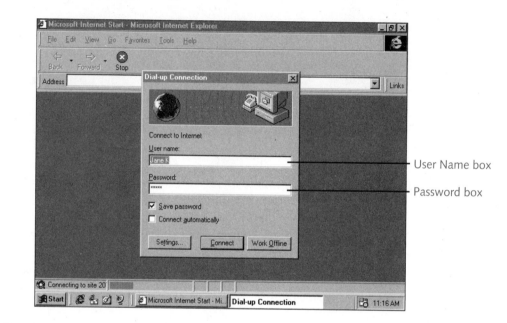

User Name box

Password box

Your ISP either supplies you with a username and password or allows you to choose your own. Contact your ISP for more information.

2   In the User Name box, be sure that your username is correct.

3   In the Password box, type your password.

4   Click the Connect button.

Your modem dials the phone number to your Internet Service Provider and connects to the Internet Service Provider's computer. Then your home page is loaded.

Navigating buttons   Address bar

Toolbar

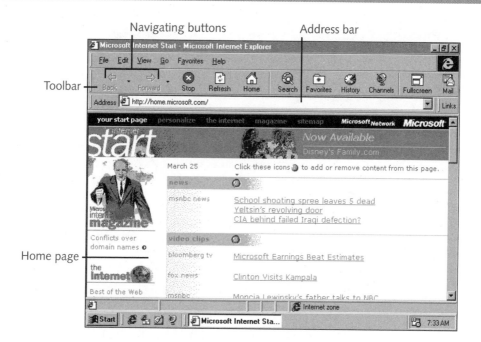

Home page

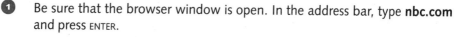

Understanding Networks   5

Load Web pages and browse a Web site

In this exercise, you visit Web sites for a few news agencies. At CNN.com, you use links and the browser window buttons to explore the Web site.

1 Be sure that the browser window is open. In the address bar, type **nbc.com** and press ENTER.

The NBC Web page is loaded in the browser window.

2 Click the Maximize button.

The browser window expands.

3 In the address bar, type **cnn.com** and press ENTER.

The CNN home page is loaded in the browser window.

4 On the CNN Interactive News navigator bar, click World.

The browser window loads the World News main page.

5 On the Standard toolbar, click the Back button.

The browser window returns to the CNN.com home page.

6 Continue viewing the articles on the CNN Web site. When you are finished, click the Home button.

The browser window displays your home page.

Finding a particular Web page or Web site

The World Wide Web contains so much information that sometimes you need help finding information on a particular topic. The Search button on the browser window opens a Search pane with access to several Web search engines. A *search engine* is a program on the Internet that allows you to search for Web pages by typing keywords or browsing topics. When you type a keyword in the search box and start the search, the search engine searches the Web and displays a list of Web sites that contain your keyword. You can use a keyword that is as general or as specific as you want. If the list of Web sites is too long, you might want to use a more specific word or use a phrase.

Imagine your client is interested in expanding his or her gardening business to include endangered plants. You search the Web using the phrase "endangered plants."

Use a search engine to find a Web site

In this exercise, you search for a Web site using a search engine. The search engine used in this exercise is Infoseek. However, if Infoseek is not responding you can achieve similar results if you use another service.

 1   Be sure that the browser window is open. On the Standard toolbar, click the Search button.

The Search pane appears on the left side of the window.

2   Click the Choose a Search Engine link, and then click Infoseek.

The Search pane displays the Infoseek search engine.

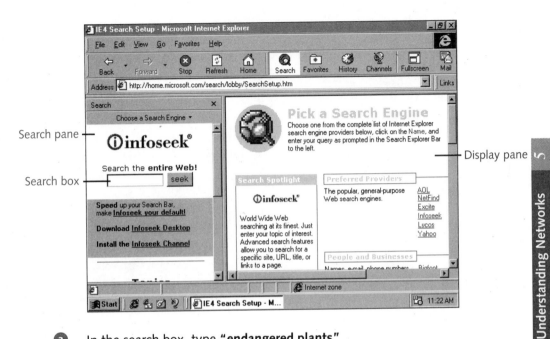

Search pane

Search box

Display pane

③ In the search box, type **"endangered plants"**

The quotes force the search engine to look for the entire phrase "endangered plants." If you don't use the quotes, the search engine will look for Web sites that include the word "endangered" or the word "plants."

For more information about the security alert message, see the sidebar after this exercise.

④ In the Search pane, click the Seek button.

A message informing you that you are about to send information to the Internet and it might be possible for other people to see what you are sending is displayed.

⑤ Click Yes.

Infoseek searches for Web pages and articles containing the phrase "endangered plants." The results appear in the Search pane.

⑥ In the Search pane, scroll down until you see the National Collection of Endangered Plants link.

⑦ Click the National Collection of Endangered Plants link.

If you see more than one National Collection of Endangered Plants link, click the first one in the results list. The browser window loads the National Collection of Endangered Plants page, and it appears in the Display pane.

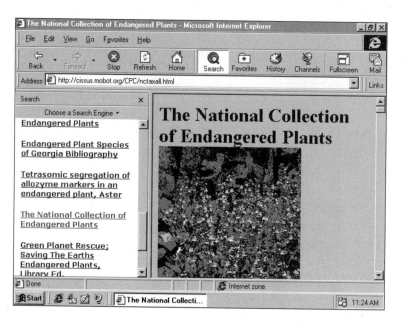

8 On the Standard toolbar, click the Search button.

The Search pane closes, and the Display pane expands to fill the browser window.

Security Alert

When you send information to someone via the Internet, the information might be passed through several computers before it reaches the recipient's computer. If the information stops at another computer, it could be read by someone other than the person you intended. When you send the information, before it leaves your computer, you will be reminded of the possibility of having someone else read the information. The security alert message is a reminder of this possibility.

If you use your credit card to buy something from a company on the Internet, you should be aware that your credit card number might be read by someone else. Some companies provide a secure site for people who make purchases from them. When a site is secured, your information is encrypted and can't be read by other people. A site is secure if there is a padlock icon on the gray bar at the bottom of the browser window or if the company's address in the address bar begins with the letters "https."

Keeping track of your favorite Web pages

Once you find a Web page that is particularly useful and you intend to revisit it, you can add the Web page to your Favorites menu. You can open your favorite Web sites by clicking them in the Favorites menu. You don't need to open a browser and remember the Web page address or the path to the Web page. For example, you have a client who develops video games. When new technology becomes available to the public, your client needs to know about it. You can keep track of new technology by adding one of the technology news Web sites to your Favorites menu.

Add a Web page to the Favorites menu

For a demonstration of how to add a Web site to your Favorites menu, in the AVIFiles folder on the Microsoft Windows 98 Step by Step CD-ROM, double-click the page123 icon.

In this exercise, you visit the PC World Web site and add it to your Favorites menu.

1 Be sure that the browser window is open. In the address bar, type **pcworld.com** and press ENTER.

The browser window loads the PC World home page.

2 On the Favorites menu, click Add To Favorites.

The Add Favorite dialog box appears.

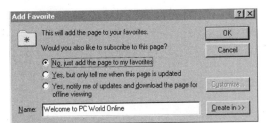

3 Click OK.

The Add Favorite dialog box closes.

4 On the menu bar, click Favorites.

A shortcut to the PC World Web page appears on the Favorites menu. To go to the PC World Web site, you click this link on the Favorites menu.

5 Press the ESC key.

The Favorites menu closes.

Subscribing to Web pages

Sometimes, you need to monitor the changes to a particular Web page. For example, if one of your clients sold toys, you might find it useful to keep up to date on trends in the toy industry by monitoring a toy industry Web page. Rather than check for changes to the Web page every day, you can subscribe to the Web page. Subscribing to a Web page allows you to see what has changed on the Web page without actually visiting the Web page.

When you subscribe to a Web page, the browser program checks whether there were changes made to the page since the last time you looked at it. You can set the subscription to notify you of changes or to copy the new page to your hard disk for later viewing. This is very useful if you use a laptop and need current information while you are traveling. Before leaving the office, you can update your subscriptions to download any new information to your laptop and then review the new information while you are on a plane or in a meeting with a client. This process is also helpful when you are at home and don't want to stay connected to the Internet.

Subscribe to a Web page

When you subscribe to a Web page, no payment is involved. Subscribing means that you request update information about the Web page.

In this exercise, you visit a Web page and then subscribe to the Web page.

1 Be sure that the browser window is open. In the address bar, type **www.toysource.com/events.htm** and press ENTER.

The browser window loads the Toysource Calendar of Worldwide Events page.

2 On the Favorites menu, click Add To Favorites.

The Add Favorite dialog box appears.

3 Select the Yes But Only Tell Me When This Page Is Updated option.

You will only receive a notification when the page is updated. The browser will not download the page to your hard disk.

4 Click the Customize button.

The Subscription Wizard dialog box appears.

5 Select the Yes, Send An E-mail To The Following Address option.

6 Click the Change Address button.

The Mail Options dialog box appears.

7 In the E-mail Address box, type your e-mail address, and then press TAB.

8 In the E-mail Server Name box, type your e-mail server address.

If you don't know what your e-mail server address is, you can contact your system administrator. If you are at home, you can contact your ISP for the e-mail server address.

9 Click OK.

The Mail Options dialog box closes.

10 Click Next.

11 Be sure that the No option is selected, and then click Finish.

The Add Favorites dialog box appears.

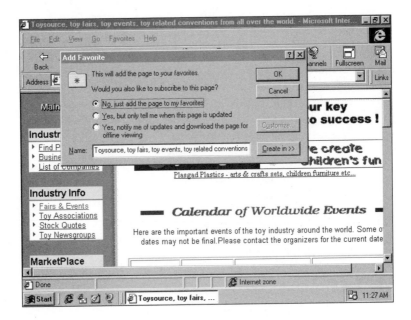

12 In the Name box, select the text, and then type **Toy Conventions**

The shortcut name is changed to Toy Conventions.

13 Click OK.

The Add Favorite dialog box closes. When the Web page is updated, you will be notified. If you want to change the setting, see the "Scheduling Your Subscription Updates" sidebar following this exercise.

14 On the Standard toolbar, click the Favorites button.

The Favorites pane appears on the left side of the browser window with a shortcut to the Toy Conventions Web page.

15 On the Standard toolbar, click the Favorites button.

The Favorites pane closes, and the Display pane expands to fill the browser window.

Update Web page subscriptions

1 Be sure that the browser window is open. On the Favorites menu, click Update All Subscriptions.

The browser checks all Web page subscriptions and alerts you of pages changed since the last update.

2 Close the browser window.

Scheduling Your Subscription Updates

Once you subscribe to a Web page, you might want to change how often you receive updates or how you are notified about updates. You can change the subscription settings so the updates occur daily, weekly, or at an interval you choose. When you change your subscription settings, you can also change how you want to be notified or if you want the update to be downloaded to your computer so you can view it at a later time.

Change the frequency of the updates

1 On the Favorites menu, click Manage Subscriptions.

The Subscriptions window opens, and a list of your subscriptions is displayed.

2 Right-click the subscription you want to change.

3 Click Properties.

The Properties dialog box appears.

4 Click the Schedule tab.

5 Click the Scheduled down arrow, and then click Weekly.

6 Click the Edit button.

The Custom Schedule dialog box appears.

7 Select the Wednesday check box, and then clear any other day check boxes.

The updates will be scheduled to happen every Wednesday.

8 In the Update At box, click the up arrow once.

Your subscription will be updated every Wednesday at the new time.

9 Click OK.

The dialog box closes.

10 Click OK.

The Properties dialog box closes.

11 Close the Subscriptions window.

Sending and Receiving E-mail with Outlook Express

New!

Like many companies, your public relations firm is looking forward to communicating with co-workers and clients via e-mail. Electronic messaging, or e-mail, is the fastest growing form of corporate and personal communication. With Outlook Express, you can address, compose, and send a message to one or many individuals.

When Inbox is selected, the Outlook Express window is divided into three panes. The Folder pane on the left lists folders in which to store your messages. Outlook Express uses the first five folders to manage incoming and outgoing mail. The Message List pane in the upper right displays the contents of the folder selected in the Folder pane. Finally, the Message Contents pane in the lower right displays the text of the message selected in the Message List pane. When you open Microsoft Outlook Express, your screen displays several shortcuts that help you locate the tasks you want to perform.

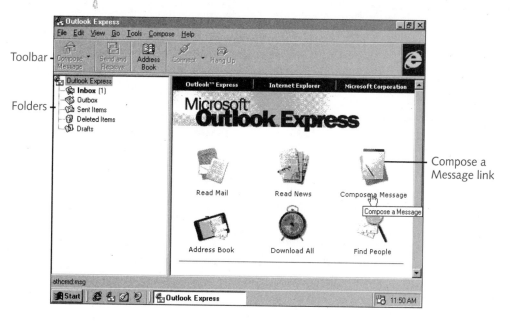

Compose and send a message

To practice using Outlook Express you will compose and send a message. So that everyone using this book can follow the same directions, you'll send the message to a fictitious person. If you want, you can send the message to someone else if you know his or her e-mail address.

Outlook Express

① On the Desktop, click the Outlook Express icon.

The Outlook Express window opens.

② Click the Compose Message link.

The New Message window opens.

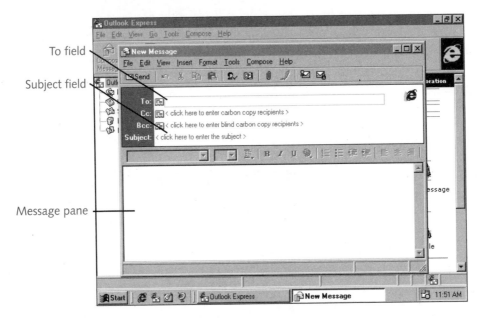

If you sent a message to the fictitious person, you will receive a message informing you that the e-mail was undeliverable. Your message was undeliverable because the e-mail address doesn't exist.

③ In the To field, type **johnsi@mightyflight.com**

If you are sending an e-mail message to someone else, type his or her e-mail address in the To field.

④ Press TAB three times.

⑤ In the Subject field, type **Monday's Meeting**

⑥ Press TAB.

⑦ In the message pane, type **We're set to meet on Monday to discuss the new super action toy.**

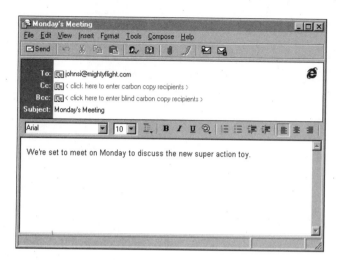

If you are connected to a network, your messages will automatically be received and sent.

8   Click the Send button.

The New Message window closes. The message moves to the Outbox folder.

9   Click the Send And Receive button.

The message is sent and is moved to your Sent Items folder.

Receiving, reading, and replying to an e-mail message

When you receive messages, they are stored in your Inbox folder. You can tell how many unread messages you have by looking at the number next to the Inbox folder.

Your Inbox screen is divided into two parts. The upper part of the screen is called the Message List pane and shows the subject and author of the messages you have received. The lower part of the screen is called the Message Contents pane and shows the text of the message. As you click each message in the Message List pane, the contents of the message appear in the Message Contents pane. You can quickly scan your messages to determine which ones you want to read.

There are two methods to reply to the e-mail messages you receive. You can create a message from scratch, or you can directly reply to the sender. When you reply to a message, you can reply to just the sender or to all the recipients of the original message. You can also include the original message you received as well as your reply. You can forward the message to another person who did not receive the original.

Receive a message

● Click the Send/Receive button.

The computer connects to your network e-mail server or to the Internet and retrieves incoming messages and places them in the Inbox folder. Any messages in your Outbox folder will be sent. The Outbox is used to hold messages that are ready to be sent.

Read a message

In this exercise, you read the "Welcome to Microsoft Outlook Express" message.

1 Be sure that the Outlook Express window is open. In the Folder pane, click the Inbox folder.

The contents of the Inbox folder are displayed in the Message List pane.

2 In the Message List pane, click the message with the subject "Welcome to Microsoft Outlook Express."

The contents of the "Welcome to Microsoft Outlook Express" message are displayed in the Message Contents pane.

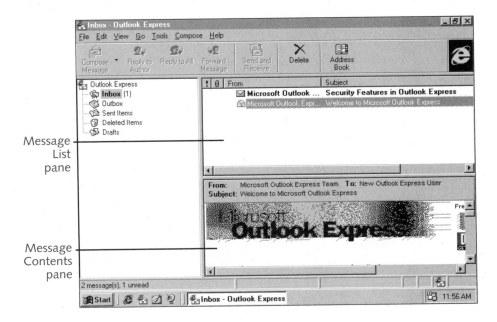

Message List pane

Message Contents pane

③ In the Message List pane, double-click the "Welcome to Microsoft Outlook Express" message.

The Welcome to Microsoft Outlook Express window opens.

④ Close the Welcome to Microsoft Outlook Express message window.

Reply to a message

In this exercise, you practice replying to a message in your Inbox.

① Be sure that the Outlook Express window is open. Click the Inbox folder.

The contents of the Inbox folder are displayed in the Message List pane.

② In the Message List pane, select a message.

The message window opens.

You don't have to open a message to reply to the message. You can select the message and then click the Reply To Author button on the Standard toolbar.

③ Click the Reply To Author button.

The message header contains the original message author and subject. In addition, the message body includes a copy of the original message.

 In the message pane, type a message.

5 Click the Send button.

The Reply message moves to your Outbox. If you are not connected to a network, you will need to click the Send And Receive button to send your message.

Working Offline to Compose and Read Messages

If your business requires you to travel and use a laptop, it can be difficult to remain connected to the Internet for the extended period of time needed to compose and read all of your e-mail. Since all of your messages, both incoming and outgoing, are saved on your hard disk, you can work on your e-mail offline. When you are offline, you are not connected to the Internet. When you reconnect to the Internet, Outlook Express sends the messages in your Outbox folder and copies incoming messages to your Inbox folder.

Work offline in Outlook Express

1. In the Outlook Express window, on the File menu, click Work Offline.

2. On the Standard toolbar, click the Compose New Messages button.

3. In the To field, type the recipient's name, and then press TAB.

4. In the Subject field, type the subject of the e-mail.

5. In the message pane, type the message, and then click the Send button.

   When you click the Send button, the message is moved to the Outbox folder. You will see a message informing you that the message will stay in your Outbox until you click the Send And Receive button.

6. On the File menu, click Send And Receive.

   Outlook Express will reconnect to the Internet, and your message will be sent.

Read and reply to messages

1. On the Standard toolbar, click the Send And Receive button to receive any new messages.

2. On the File menu, click Work Offline.

3. In the Folder pane, click the Inbox folder.

4. To view a message, click the message in the Message List pane.

   The message is displayed in the Message Contents pane.

5. To reply to the message, on the Standard toolbar, click the Reply To Author button.

   A window opens with the person's name in the To field and the original message attached.

6. Type your reply, and then click Send.

   When you click the Send button, the reply message is moved to the Outbox folder.

7. When you are ready to reconnect to the Internet, on the Standard toolbar, click the Connect button.

   The computer establishes a connection with the Internet.

Understanding Networks

5

<table>
<tr><td>One Step Further</td><td></td></tr>
</table>

Deleting Messages

When you delete a message, the message moves to the Deleted Items folder. Like the Recycle Bin, the Deleted Items folder stores messages until you empty the folder. If you don't want to empty the folder manually, you can customize the Deleted Items folder to empty the deleted messages every time you close the Outlook Express program.

Imagine one of your partners is retiring at the end of the month. Your co-workers have decided to throw a going away party for him. E-mails are sent throughout the month asking for gift suggestions or reminding everyone of the party. You delete the messages after you read them. However, you don't want to empty the Deleted Items folder every time you delete messages, so you decide to change your Outlook Express options to delete the messages in the folder when you close Outlook Express.

Delete a message

1   Be sure that the Outlook Express window is open. In the Folder pane, click the Inbox folder.

The contents of the Inbox folder are displayed in the Message List pane.

2   In the Message List pane, click the message you want to delete.

3   On the Standard toolbar, click the Delete button.

The message moves to the Deleted Items folder.

4   Click the Deleted Items folder.

The contents of the Deleted Items folder are displayed in the Message List pane. This message will be deleted in the next step.

5   Right-click the Deleted Items folder.

A shortcut menu is displayed. If you only want to delete one file from the Deleted Items folder, right-click the file, and then Delete.

6   Click Empty Folder.

A message asking you to confirm the deletion is displayed.

7   Click Yes.

The messages in the Deleted Items folder are removed entirely from Outlook Express.

Change your folder options to empty the Deleted Items folder when you close Outlook Express

1 Be sure that the Outlook Express window is open. On the Tools menu, click Options.

The Options dialog box appears, and the General tab is active.

2 Select the Empty Messages From The Deleted Items Folder On Exit check box.

3 Click OK.

The option is set, and when you exit Outlook Express, any messages in the Deleted Items folder will be deleted.

Finish the lesson

1 To continue to the next lesson, delete commands added to the Favorites menu during the lesson. Right-click the command, click Delete, and then click Yes.

2 Delete unwanted messages from Outlook Express. Click the message, and then click the Delete button.

3 If you are finished using your computer for now, click the Start button, and then click Shut Down.

The Shut Down Windows dialog box appears.

4 Select the Shut Down option, and click OK.

The Windows 98 logo appears as the computer shuts down.

Understanding Networks

5

Lesson 5 Quick Reference

To	Do this
Open the browser window	On the Quick Launch toolbar on the taskbar, click the Launch Internet Explorer Browser button.
Load Web pages and browse a Web site	Open the browser window. In the address bar, type the location of the Web site, and press ENTER. Click a link on the Web page.
Use a search engine to find a Web site	Open the browser window. Click the Search button. Click the Choose Provider down arrow, and then click a search engine. In the search box, type a keyword or topic, and press ENTER. In the results list, click a link to a Web site.
Add a Web page to the Favorites menu	Open the browser window. In the address bar, type the location of the Web page, and press ENTER. When the Web page is loaded, on the Favorites menu, click Add To Favorites. Click OK.
Subscribe to a Web page	Open the browser window. In the address bar, type the location of the Web page, and press ENTER. When the Web page loads, on the Favorites menu, click Add To Favorites. Click the Yes But Only Tell Me When This Page Is Updated option. In the Name box, type a name for the subscription. Click OK.
Update all of your Web page subscriptions	Open the browser window. On the Favorites menu, click Update All Subscriptions.
Compose and send an e-mail message	Click the Outlook Express icon. Click the Compose Message link. Type the name of the recipient. Press TAB three times, and then type the subject of the e-mail. Press TAB, and then type the message. When you have finished typing your message, click the Send button, and then, if your computer is not attached to a network, click the Send And Receive button.

Lesson 5 Quick Reference

To	Do this
Receive e-mail if your computer is not attached to a network	In Outlook Express, click the Send/Receive button.
Read an e-mail message	In the Message List pane, click the message, and then in the Message Contents pane, read the message. *or* In the Message List pane, double-click the message.
Reply to an e-mail message	In the message window, click the Reply To Author button. In the message pane, type your reply. Click the Send button. If your computer is not attached to a network, click the Send And Receive button.
Work on e-mail while disconnected from the Internet	In Outlook Express, on the File menu, click Work Offline.
Delete an e-mail message	In the Message List pane, click the message. Click the Delete button.
Empty the Deleted Items folder	In Outlook Express, right-click the Deleted Items folder. Click Empty Folder. Click Yes.

Understanding Networks

5

Review & Practice

You will review and practice how to:

✔ *Visit and browse a World Wide Web site.*

✔ *Search for Web pages on topics of personal or business interest.*

✔ *Subscribe to a Web page so that you can get updated information.*

✔ *Compose and send e-mail messages using Outlook Express.*

✔ *Read and reply to incoming e-mail messages.*

ESTIMATED TIME
20 min.

Before you move on to Part 3, which covers upgrades and regular maintenance in Microsoft Windows 98, you can practice the skills you learned in Part 2 by working through this Review & Practice section. You will use the browser window to visit Web sites on the Internet and send and receive e-mail with Microsoft Outlook Express.

Scenario

A partner wants to learn how to use the Internet to do research for a marketing campaign and to exchange e-mail with a client. You introduce your partner to the features of the browser window, and you show him how to search for, browse, and subscribe to Web sites. You also demonstrate how to use Outlook Express to compose and send an e-mail message. Finally, you read an incoming message and reply to the sender.

Step 1:   **Open the Browser Window and View a Web Site**

Your partner is trying to learn more about the travel business in an effort to win a new account. You suggest that some research on existing travel agencies already doing business on the World Wide Web might provide excellent material for a marketing plan proposal. You open the browser window and visit a trade association supporting the travel industry.

1   Use the taskbar to open the browser window.

2   Visit the National Business Travel Association Web site at http://www.nbta.org

3   Click the About the NBTA link to learn more about the National Business Travel Association.

For more information about	See
Opening the browser window	Lesson 5
Visiting a Web site	Lesson 5
Browsing a Web site	Lesson 5

Step 2:   **Search for and Subscribe to Web Pages**

While the NBTA provided useful information, your partner is interested specifically in excursion travel for divers since his client specializes in diving locales and services. You use the Yahoo search engine to find Web pages specifically relating to dive travel. You then subscribe to a Web page that your partner wants to visit at a later date.

1   Display the Search pane, and then switch to the Yahoo search engine.

2   Search for the words "dive" and "travel."

3   Visit the Dive Travel Planner Web page from the list of available links.

4   Subscribe to the Dive Travel Planner Web page.

For more information about	See
Using a search engine to find a Web site	Lesson 5
Subscribing to a Web site	Lesson 5

Step 3:   Compose and Send E-mail

After exploring several dive industry Web sites, your partner is excited about setting up a meeting with his prospective client. Apparently, this client prefers communicating via e-mail, so your partner wants you to show him how to compose and send an e-mail message.

1   Use the taskbar to start Outlook Express.

2   Compose a new message addressed to your e-mail address with the subject "Lunch Next Week To Talk About Online Marketing Ideas."

tip

Normally you wouldn't send a message to yourself. However, in this Review & Practice, you will send a message to your e-mail address and then respond to the message.

3   Compose the body of the message requesting a prospective client to meet for lunch next week to talk about marketing a dive travel agency on the Web.

4   Send the message.

For more information about	See
Starting Outlook Express	Lesson 5
Addressing an e-mail message	Lesson 5
Sending a message	Lesson 5

Step 4:   Receive and Reply to E-mail

A few hours later, your partner receives an e-mail message from his prospective client. You demonstrate how to read and reply to the message.

1   In Outlook Express, locate the "Lunch Next Week To Talk About Online Marketing Ideas" message in your Inbox.

2   Read the message.

3   Reply to the message, indicating that Thursday at 1:30 P.M. would be fine for lunch and suggesting Salty's on the Sound for a restaurant.

4   Delete the "Lunch Next Week To Talk About Online Marketing Ideas" message from your Inbox.

For more information about	See
Reading and replying to an e-mail message	Lesson 5
Deleting e-mail messages	Lesson 5

Finish the Review & Practice

❶ Close the browser and Outlook Express windows.

❷ If you are finished using your computer for now, click the Start button, and then click Shut Down.

The Shut Down Windows dialog box appears.

❸ Select the Shut Down option, and click OK.

The Windows 98 logo appears as the computer shuts down.

PART 3

Improving Performance

6

Improving Speed, Efficiency, and Accessibility

**ESTIMATED
TIME
40 min.**

In this lesson you will learn how to:

✔ *Improve the way your hard disk stores information.*

✔ *Schedule regular maintenance to keep your computer running efficiently.*

✔ *Use power management settings to keep energy use minimal.*

✔ *Make the computer easier to use for people with disabilities.*

In the past, your firm has relied on outside consultants to fix small computer problems and to improve hardware and software performance. With Windows 98, you can use the maintenance tools to accomplish enhancements and tune-ups without having to rely on an outside consultant. Some of the tools are "one-time" implementations, such as converting your hard drive to a FAT32 format, while other tools allow you to run tasks as needed.

In this lesson, you will walk through the steps of "one-time only "computer improvements. You will learn about when and why to run Windows 98 Maintenance tools, which is just as important as learning the actual steps. If you work in a corporate setting, you might find that the commands described in this lesson have already been executed or have been disabled.

Converting to FAT32 to Increase Hard Drive Capacity

Your computer uses a File Allocation Table (FAT) to store information about files. The File Allocation Table is a list maintained by Windows 98 to keep track of how and where your files are stored on your hard disk. The previous versions of operating programs used a FAT16 format, while Windows 98 allows you to use a FAT32 format. FAT32 is an improvement of the FAT16 format. When your hard drive is in FAT32 format, your files are stored more efficiently, allowing you to use all of your disk space. In addition, your programs might run from 18 to 48 percent faster and use fewer resources, such as memory, thereby improving your computer's performance. You can convert your hard drive to the FAT32 format by using the Drive Converter (FAT32) Wizard.

With the advantages of converting to FAT32 why do some companies and individuals choose not to convert? One reason is that some software programs won't run with FAT32. For example, some companies might have custom software that was developed a few years ago and the software hasn't been upgraded. Another reason for not converting to FAT32 is that you cannot use a disk compression program with a FAT32 format. A disk compression program compresses your files so you have more space.

Some companies might disable the Drive Converter (FAT32) Wizard until the entire company is ready to convert to a FAT32 format. For example, before your firm upgraded to Windows 98, some employees were working on computers with MS-DOS, while other employees were working on computers with Windows 3.1 or Windows 95. In a mixed environment like this, it is a good idea to disable the Drive Converter (FAT32) Wizard until everyone is working with Windows 98.

If your entire organization is upgrading to FAT32 or you use your computer at home with software that has been released two years prior to the release of Windows 98 or less, the advantages of the new file system probably outweighs any disadvantages.

important

Once you convert to FAT32, there is no program in Windows 98 for converting back to FAT16.

Use the Drive Converter (FAT32) Wizard to convert your hard drive

In this exercise, you walk through the Drive Converter (FAT32) Wizard. The conversion process can take several hours.

See Lesson 7, "Using Windows 98 Tools," for information about using the Microsoft Backup program.

important

As a safety precaution, you should make a backup of any important data you have and make a Windows 98 Emergency Startup disk before making any major changes to your hard drive. See Appendix B to make a Windows 98 Emergency Startup disk. If you use disk compression or utility programs, such as Norton Utilities, McAfee, or PCTools, you need to disable the programs before you start the conversion wizard. After completing the conversion, check with the manufacturer of the program for compatibility with FAT32.

1. Click the Start button, point to Programs, and then point to Accessories.

2. On the Accessories menu, point to System Tools, and then click Drive Converter (FAT32).

   The Drive Converter (FAT32) dialog box appears.

3. Click the Next button.

   A list of drives that can be converted to FAT32 is displayed.

4. To select the drive to convert, click the Drive down arrow, and then click the drive letter you want to convert.

   If there is only one drive, there is no down arrow available and you can skip this step.

5. Click Next.

   A message is displayed, warning that if you are running MS-DOS, a previous version of Windows, or Windows NT, you will not be able to access a FAT32 drive while running those operating systems. For example, if you have Windows 98 and Windows NT installed on the same computer, you will not be able use the FAT32 drive with Windows NT.

6. Click OK.

   The converter wizard checks for incompatible programs. If any are found, then you are warned to disable or uninstall them before starting the Drive Converter.

Improving System Efficiency   6

7 Click Next.

You are asked if you would like to back up your files before converting. If you want to back up your files, click the Create Backup button. The Microsoft Backup program starts.

8 Click Next.

You are informed that the computer will restart in MS-DOS mode.

9 Click Next.

Your computer is restarted in MS-DOS mode. The Drive Converter (FAT32) Wizard runs the ScanDisk program, and then the wizard starts the disk conversion. When the converter wizard is finished, it restarts your computer and starts the Disk Defragmenter program. The Disk Defragmenter might take several hours, depending on the size of your hard drive. A message informing you that the conversion is complete is displayed.

10 Click Finish.

The Drive Converter (FAT32) dialog box closes.

Scheduling Regular Computer Maintenance

Prior to upgrading to Windows 98, you had to spent part of your day going through your folders and deleting files that you no longer needed or running Disk Defragmenter to improve your computer speed. One of the advantages of upgrading to Windows 98 is using the Maintenance Wizard. The wizard establishes a regular schedule for basic software maintenance, which makes sure that your computer performs at its best. You only need to run the Maintenance Wizard once to create a regular maintenance schedule. When you complete the wizard, you can immediately run the maintenance tasks or wait until the next regularly scheduled time. The computer must be on during scheduled maintenance tasks and maintenance might take from 15 minutes to two hours to complete.

There are three maintenance tools to help you keep your computer running efficiently: ScanDisk, Disk Defragmenter, and Disk Cleanup. The following table briefly describes each maintenance tool.

Maintenance tool	Description
ScanDisk	Detects and, where possible, repairs problems on the hard disk.
Disk Defragmenter	Rearranges files and unused space on your hard disk so that programs run faster.
Disk Cleanup	Frees space on your hard disk by locating and removing temporary and unnecessary files that can be safely deleted.

Use the Maintenance Wizard to schedule regular maintenance

In this exercise, you use the Maintenance Wizard to schedule a nightly run of all the maintenance tasks.

1 Click the Start button, point to Programs, and then point to Accessories.

2 On the Accessories menu, point to System Tools, and then click Maintenance Wizard.

The Maintenance Wizard dialog box appears.

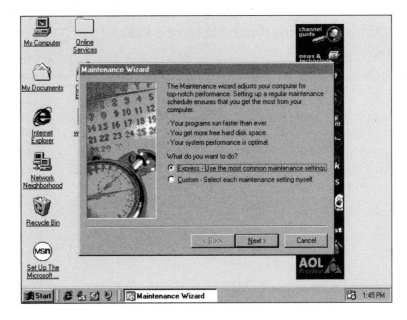

3 Click the Express option, and then click the Next button.

The scheduling options are displayed, and you are asked to select a maintenance schedule.

4 Select the Nights - Midnight to 3:00 AM option, and then click Next.

The Maintenance task list is displayed with a reminder to leave your computer on so the maintenance can occur.

5 If you would like to immediately perform maintenance, select the When I Click Finish Perform Each Scheduled Task For The First Time check box, and then click Finish. Otherwise, click Finish.

The Maintenance Wizard will perform all three tune-up tasks immediately after you click Finish. Otherwise, the tune-up tasks will not be run until the next regularly scheduled time.

important

You must leave your computer on for scheduled maintenance tasks to function. If your computer is turned off, the scheduled maintenance tasks will not run until the next scheduled date.

View scheduled maintenance tasks

You have run the Maintenance Wizard, but now you want to review the time the tasks are to run. In this exercise, you use the Task Scheduler to view the time and tasks you chose.

Task Scheduler

1 On the taskbar, double-click the Task Scheduler icon.

The Scheduled Tasks window opens.

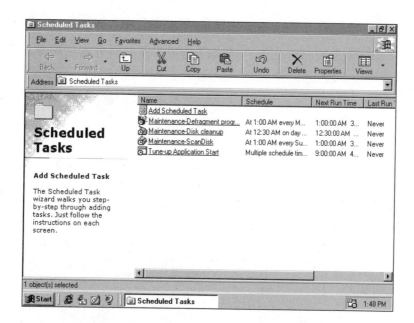

Maximize

2 To see the entire schedule, click the Maximize button.

3 Right-click a blank area in the Scheduled Tasks window.

A shortcut menu is displayed.

4 Point to View, and then click Details.

The details of each scheduled task are displayed.

5 Point to Maintenance–Disk Cleanup.

The schedule for running the Maintenance–Disk Cleanup task is displayed on the left side of the Scheduled Tasks window.

6 Point to Maintenance–ScanDisk.

The schedule for the Maintenance–ScanDisk task is displayed on the left side of the Scheduled Tasks window.

7 Close the Scheduled Tasks window.

Improving System Efficiency   6

Reschedule a maintenance task

You want to reschedule one of your tasks. In this exercise, you reschedule the disk cleanup to take place every 13 days.

For a demonstration of how to reschedule a maintenance task, in the AVIFiles folder on the Microsoft Windows 98 Step by Step CD-ROM, double-click the page152 icon.

1 On the taskbar, double-click the Task Scheduler icon.

2 Click Maintenance–Disk Cleanup.

The Maintenance–Disk Cleanup dialog box appears.

3 Click the Schedule tab.

The current schedule for the disk cleanup is displayed.

4 Click the Schedule Task down arrow, and then click Daily.

5 In the Schedule Task Daily area, click in the Every box, and type **13**

6 Click OK.

The Maintenance–Disk Cleanup dialog box closes. The disk cleanup task will run every 13 days at 12:30 A.M.

If you don't see the revised schedule, press F5 to refresh your screen.

7 Point to Maintenance–Disk Cleanup.

The revised schedule for running the Disk Cleanup tune-up procedure is displayed in the left pane.

8 Close the Scheduled Tasks window.

The disk cleanup will run at the next scheduled time.

Changing System Settings to Improve Energy Efficiency

Windows 98 suits your firm because it includes ways to adapt computers to special conditions and needs. For example, some of your co-workers have laptops or work at home, where saving battery power or reducing the electric bill is an important consideration.

Windows 98 includes a program you can use to reduce the amount of energy used by your computer. For example, if you don't use your keyboard or mouse for a period of time, you can choose to have your computer go into standby mode. When you computer goes into standby mode, the monitor screen goes blank and your hard drive stops spinning. When you press any key on the keyboard or move the mouse, the computer immediately returns to the same screen as before it went to standby. Another option is to have the computer go into standby at a specific time you set. Scheduled tasks, such as computer maintenance and Web page updates, bring the computer back to full power at the scheduled time and then return it to standby again when the tasks are complete.

During the recent upgrade, your firm purchased three laptops to lend to employees who travel. One of the employees leaves the laptop on for long periods of time even if he is not using it. This causes the battery to die quicker. You show him how to change the power management settings so that the laptop can go into standby when he isn't using it.

Modify power management settings

In this exercise, you shorten the inactive time before the monitor turns off and the computer goes into standby. The preset time is 15 minutes for your monitor and 30 minutes for your hard drive.

❶   Click the Start button, point to Settings, and then click Control Panel.
The Control Panel window opens.

❷   On the vertical scroll bar, click the down arrow until you see the Power Management icon, and then click the Power Management icon.
The Power Management Properties dialog box appears.

3 Click the System Standby down arrow, and then click After 10 Mins.

4 Click the Turn Off Monitor down arrow, and then click After 5 Mins.

5 Click OK.

The Power Management Properties dialog box closes.

6 Close the Control Panel window.

The next time your co-worker doesn't use the mouse or keyboard on the laptop for five minutes, the monitor will turn off. After 10 minutes, the computer will go into standby. To reactivate the computer and turn on the monitor, move the mouse or press a key on the keyboard. No files or data will be lost since only the monitor turns off.

Making the Computer Easier to Use for People with Disabilities

Changing the accessibility options in Windows 98 can make it easier for you to operate your computer without installing special software. The following table briefly describes the options available.

Enable the accessibility option	If you want to
StickyKeys	Use the SHIFT, CTRL, or ALT key by pressing one key at a time instead of pressing these keys in combination with other keys to perform a task.
FilterKeys	Have Windows ignore brief or repeated keystrokes, or adjust the keyboard rate, which is the rate at which a key repeats when you hold it down.
ToggleKeys	Hear tones when pressing the CAPS LOCK, NUM LOCK, and SCROLL LOCK keys.
SoundSentry	See visual warnings when your computer makes a sound.
ShowSounds	Have programs display captions for the speech and sounds they make.
High Contrast	Have programs change the color scheme to a high-contrast scheme and increase legibility whenever possible.
MouseKeys	Control the mouse pointer with the numeric keypad on your keyboard.
SerialKey Devices	Use an alternate input device for access to keyboard and mouse features.

To set accessibility options, you will use the Accessibility Wizard. Since many people might not need this wizard, it is not automatically installed. Therefore, you must first install the Accessibility Wizard from the Windows 98 CD-ROM.

Install the Accessibility Wizard

In this exercise, you install the Accessibility Wizard. You must have the Windows 98 CD-ROM to complete this exercise.

❶ Insert the Windows 98 CD-ROM in your CD-ROM drive.

❷ Click the Start button, point to Settings, and then click Control Panel.

The Control Panel window opens.

❸ Click the Add/Remove Programs icon.

The Add/Remove Programs Properties dialog box appears.

❹ Click the Windows Setup tab.

The setup program checks for installed Windows 98 components, and then a list of available programs is displayed

Improving System Efficiency **6**

⑤   Select the Accessibility check box, and click OK.

The setup program copies the files for the Accessibility Wizard from the CD-ROM to your hard disk, and a message informing you to restart your computer is displayed.

⑥   Click Yes to restart your computer.

Your computer restarts, and the new settings take effect.

⑦   Close the Control Panel window after your computer restarts.

Using the Accessibility Wizard

Once you have installed the Accessibility Wizard, you can enable any of the accessibility options. For example, if you have difficulty using a mouse, you can change your settings so you can use your keyboard to perform functions you would usually perform with a mouse.

Run the Accessibility Wizard

In this exercise, you use the Accessibility Wizard to change your settings so you can use the 10-key pad on your keyboard instead of your mouse.

❶　Click the Start button, point to Programs, point to Accessories, and then point to Accessibility.

❷　On the Accessibility menu, click Accessibility Wizard.

The Accessibility Wizard dialog box appears.

❸　Click Next.

The option to select the text size appears. You can change the size of the text for your icons, menus, window title bars, and other features. This does not change the text inside windows.

❹　Click Next.

The screen to set wizard options appears.

⑤ Select the I Have Difficulty Using The Keyboard Or Mouse option, and then click Next.

The option to select StickyKeys appears.

⑥ Be sure that the No option is selected, and then click Next.

The option to select BounceKeys appears.

⑦ Be sure that the No option is selected, and then click Next.

The option to select ToggleKeys appears.

⑧ Be sure that the No option is selected, and then click Next.

The option to receive Extra Keyboard Help appears.

⑨ Click the Yes option, and then click Next.

The option to use MouseKeys appears.

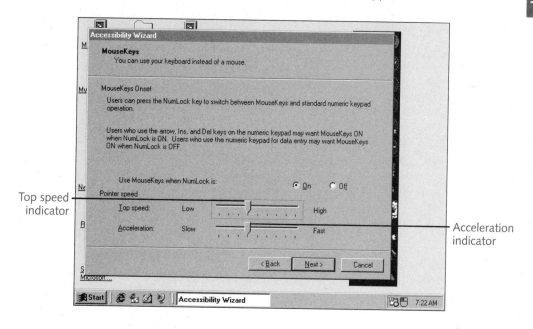

🔟 Click the Yes option, and then click Next.

You might want to write down which key to press to perform the mouse functions. The option to change the pointer speed appears.

Top speed indicator

Acceleration indicator

Improving System Efficiency 6

⓫ Be sure that the On option is selected. Drag the top speed indicator to the right.

Your mouse pointer will move more quickly when you use the arrow keys.

⓬ Drag the acceleration indicator to the third line from the right.

Your mouse pointer will move faster when you use the arrow keys on the 10-key pad. This is very useful if you have to move your mouse pointer from one side of the Desktop to the other side.

⓭ Click Next.

The option to change the size and color of your mouse pointer appears.

⓮ Click the large, white mouse pointer, and then click Next.

Your mouse pointer changes from the normal size to a large, white mouse pointer. You will then be asked with which hand you prefer to use the mouse.

⓯ If you are right-handed, be sure that the Right-handed option is selected, and then click Next. If you are left-handed, select the Left-handed option, and then click Next.

The option to change the mouse speed appears.

⑯   Click Next.

The option to have Mouse Trails appears.

⑰   Be sure that the No option is selected, and then click Next.

⑱   Click Finish.

The Accessibility Wizard dialog box closes. You can now use your 10-key pad to move your mouse pointer.

<table>
<tr><td>**One
Step
Further**</td><td># Using the 10-Key Pad
Instead of Your Mouse</td></tr>
</table>

If you completed the previous exercise, you can begin using the 10-key pad instead of your mouse. You can still use your mouse even with the new settings. This allows people to use the mouse if they don't want to use the 10-key pad.

Practice using the 10-key pad

❶   On the 10-key pad, press the UP ARROW key (the number 8 key) until your mouse pointer reaches the top of the Desktop.

❷   Press the LEFT ARROW key (the number 4 key) until your mouse pointer is over the My Computer icon.

You might have to use the RIGHT ARROW key (the number 6 key) or the DOWN ARROW key (the number 2 key) until your mouse pointer is on the My Computer icon.

❸   Once your mouse pointer is on the My Computer icon, press the number 5 key once.

The My Computer window opens.

❹   Hold down the ALT key, and then press the SPACEBAR once.

The control menu is displayed.

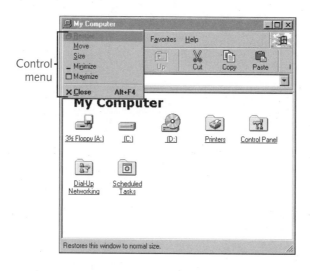

⑤ Use the arrow keys on the 10-key pad and the right SHIFT key to move the selector to Size, and press ENTER.

A four-headed arrow appears.

⑥ Press the RIGHT ARROW key that is not on the 10-key pad.

The four-headed arrow moves to the window border and turns into a two-headed arrow.

7 On the 10-key pad, press the RIGHT ARROW key (the number 6 key) until the right side of the My Computer window has increased a half an inch.

A gray border is displayed.

Gray border

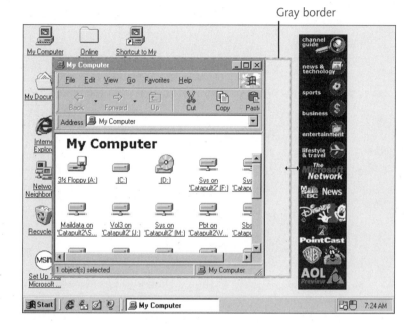

8 Press the ENTER key.

The window is resized.

9 On the 10-key pad, press the UP ARROW key (the number 8 key) until the mouse pointer reaches the My Computer title bar.

10 Press the RIGHT ARROW key (the number 6 key) until the mouse pointer is on the Close button.

You might have to use the DOWN ARROW key or the LEFT ARROW key until the mouse pointer is on the Close button.

11 Press the number 5 key.

The My Computer window closes.

Finish the lesson

1 To continue to the next lesson, close any open windows.

2 If you are finished using your computer for now, click the Start button, and then click Shut Down.

The Shut Down Windows dialog box appears.

❸   Select the Shut Down option, and click OK.

The Windows 98 logo appears as the computer shuts down.

Lesson 6 Quick Reference

To	Do this
Convert to FAT32	Click Start, point to Programs, point to Accessories, point to System Tools, and then click Drive Converter (FAT32). Click Next. Click the drive you want to convert, and then click Next. Click OK. Click Next. Click Next. Click Finish.
Schedule regular computer maintenance	Click Start, point to Programs, point to Accessories, point to System Tools, and then click Maintenance Wizard. Select the Express option, and then click Next. Select a time option, and then click Next. Click Finish.
View scheduled maintenance tasks	On the taskbar, double-click the Task Scheduler icon.
Reschedule a maintenance task	On the taskbar, double-click the Task Scheduler. Click the task to reschedule. Click the Schedule tab. Click the Schedule task arrow, and then click a time. Click OK.
Change power management settings	Click Start, point to Settings, and then click Control Panel. In the Control Panel window, click the Power Management icon. Modify the power management settings. Click OK.
Install the Accessibility Wizard	Insert the Windows 98 CD-ROM in your CD-ROM drive. Click Start, point to Settings, and then click Control Panel. Click Add/Remove Programs. Click the Windows Setup tab. Select Accessibility. Click OK
Run the Accessibility Wizard	Click Start, point to Programs, point to Accessories, point to Accessibility, and then click Accessibility Wizard. Select wizard options, and then click Next to step through the wizard. When the wizard options are complete, click Finish.

7

Using Windows 98 Tools

**ESTIMATED
TIME
40 min.**

In this lesson you will learn how to:

✔ *Connect to and set up the Update Wizard.*

✔ *Update your computer with the latest additions to Windows 98.*

✔ *Run a Windows 98 troubleshooter to fix hardware or software problems.*

✔ *Use Windows 98 tools to check your files for problems.*

✔ *Install the Microsoft Backup program and use it to keep a copy of important files and folders.*

You and your colleagues want to make sure your computers work as well as possible. If any computer problems arise, you want to be able to fix them quickly and easily. Microsoft Windows 98 contains several tools to help you accomplish these tasks. Microsoft regularly updates Windows 98 and makes these updates available on the Windows Update Web site. In addition, Windows 98 contains tools that allow you to easily fix certain computer problems. It also contains a backup program that you can use to make a copy of your key files and restore those files to your computer in the event of a major problem, such as your hard disk failing to work.

In this lesson, you will learn how to connect to the Windows Update Web site and update your computer with the most recent improvements and additions to Windows 98. Then you'll learn how to use tools in Windows 98 that help you correct the most commonly experienced computer problems. Finally, you'll learn how to install the Microsoft Backup program and use it to make backup copies of your files.

Keeping Your Windows 98 Files Current

Some companies disable Windows Update, preferring to update Windows 98 files through a network.

The technology of the computer industry changes almost daily. Microsoft addresses this issue with a program called Windows Update. Windows Update is Microsoft's new Web-based tool that helps keep your computer performing at its best by ensuring that you have the most recent additions and improvements to Windows 98. Windows Update also includes a Technical Support option that you can use to find answers to your questions.

The first time you use Windows Update, you will be prompted to install the Wizard Control and the Windows Update Wizard installation programs. Both of these programs are needed to update or restore your Windows 98 program files. You might be prompted to update these two programs as newer versions are available.

The Update Wizard scans your Windows 98 program files and then compares them to the list of current Windows 98 files on the Windows Update Web site. If any of your files are older than the ones listed on the Windows Update Web site, you will be given the option to update your older files with the newer ones.

You notice an article in a computer magazine about recent improvements to Windows 98, and you decide to run the Update Wizard to see whether any of the improvements are appropriate for you and your staff. Before you can run the wizard, you must install it. After you connect to the Windows Update Web site, you decide to gather information about the Update Wizard from the Technical Support section of the site. You want to learn more about the currently available updates. Then you run the Update Wizard to update your computer with the improvements that are useful to you and your firm.

Connect to and set up the Update Wizard

This exercise assumes you are set up to use the Internet through either a network or a dial-up connection.

In this exercise, you install and set up the Update Wizard.

1 Click the Start button, and then click Windows Update.

The browser window opens, and the Windows Update Web page is partially loaded. A message informing you that the Microsoft 98 Update Wizard Directory Finder needs to be installed is displayed.

2 Click Yes.

The Microsoft 98 Update Wizard Directory Finder is transferred, or downloaded, to your computer and installed.

Maximize

3 To see more of the Windows Update Web page content, click the Maximize button.

Your screen might not look like the picture. The content and design of the Web page shown might change.

Technical Support link

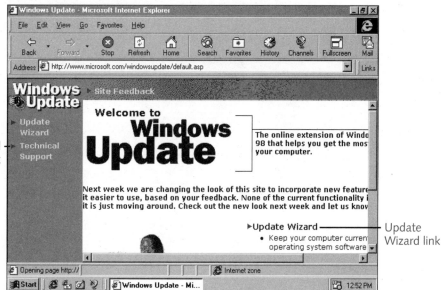

Update Wizard link

Using Windows 98 Tools

Use Windows Update to get technical support

*You must
register your
copy of
Windows 98
before you
can get
technical
support or
updates. If you
haven't regis-
tered, see Ap-
pendix B for
instructions on
how to regis-
ter.*

In this exercise, you use the Windows Update technical support link to find out more about the Update Wizard and recent improvements to Windows 98.

1 Be sure that the browser window is open with the Windows Update home page loaded. Click the Technical Support link.

The Support online search form appears.

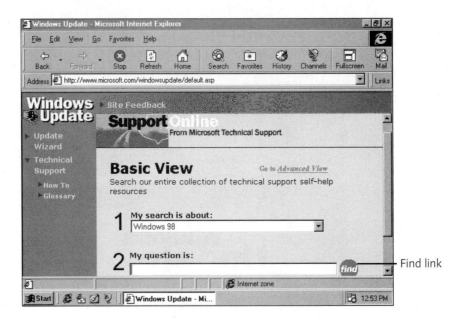

Find link

2 Click the My Search Is About down arrow, and then click Windows 98.

You can also receive help about other Microsoft products using the Support Online form.

3 In the My Question Is box, type **Update Wizard**

4 Click the Find link.

A message informing you that you are about to send information to the Internet and it might be possible for other people to see what you are sending is displayed.

5 Click Yes.

A message informing you that you will be redirected to another Web page is displayed.

6 Click Yes.

A second message informing you that you will be redirected to another Web page is displayed.

7 Click Yes.

Windows Update searches the technical support database. A list of articles containing the phrase "Update Wizard" is displayed.

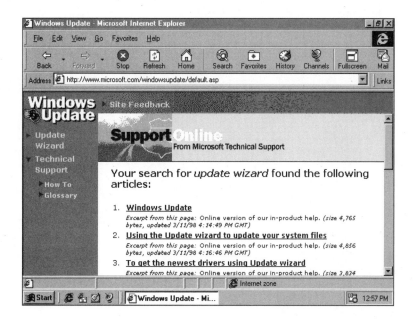

8 Click the To get the newest drivers using Update wizard link.

The contents of the article are displayed.

9 Use the scroll bar to view the contents of the article, and then click the Back button.

The list of articles is displayed.

10 Continue reading the articles. Close the browser window when you are finished reading the articles.

Run the Update Wizard

In this exercise, you run the Update Wizard to check your computer against the latest version of Windows 98.

❶ Click Start, and then click Windows Update.

The browser window opens, and the Windows Update Web page appears.

❷ Click the Update Wizard link.

Information about the Update Wizard is displayed. The Update link and the Restore link are displayed.

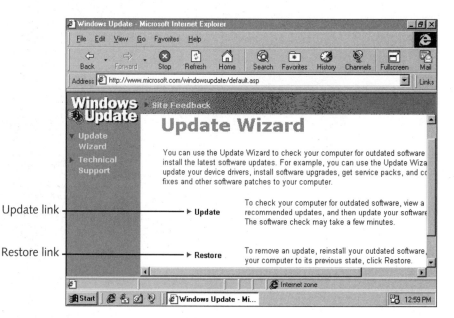

❸ Click the Update link.

A message informing you that the Windows 98 Update Wizard Control needs to be installed is displayed.

❹ Click yes

The Wizard Control is transferred, or downloaded, to your computer and installed. A message informing you that the Windows 98 Update Wizard File Install Program needs to be installed is displayed.

❺ Click yes.

The Wizard is installed. The Update Wizard searches for a list of updates and then the list of available updates is displayed.

Maximize

❻ Click the Maximize button.

7 Click the Welcome to the Windows Update Wizard link.

The description of the update is displayed in the Description pane.

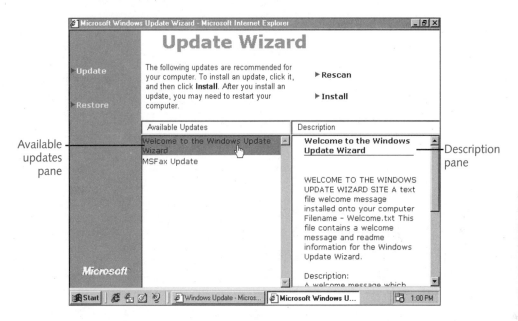

Available updates pane

Description pane

8 Click the Install link.

The Windows Update window opens and gives you the option to begin the update or to cancel.

9 Click OK.

The update is downloaded to your computer and installed.

10 Click OK when the installation process is complete.

The Update Wizard searches for more updates. If other updates are found, you can install them. If no other updates are found, a message stating that no updates were found is displayed in the Available Updates pane.

11 Close the Microsoft Windows Update Wizard window.

12 Close the browser window.

Troubleshooting Computer Problems

Often the best place to start if you experience problems with your computer is a Windows 98 troubleshooter. Troubleshooters cover a wide range of topics from software to hardware. When you use a troubleshooter, you first answer a series of questions designed to diagnose the problem. Then you follow the steps required to fix the problem.

Using Windows 98 Tools

Imagine you are having trouble printing a proposal for one of your clients. When you print your proposals, all you see is garbled characters on the page. You decide to learn more about the Windows 98 troubleshooters and then use the Print Troubleshooter to help you solve your printing problem.

Read tips about how to use Windows 98 troubleshooters

In this exercise, you read the tips for using troubleshooters and then display a list of available troubleshooters in the Help file.

1 Click the Start button, and then click Help.

The Windows Help window opens.

2 Click the Contents tab.

3 To see all the topics on the Contents tab, click the Maximize button.

4 Click Troubleshooting.

The menu expands to display the topics under Troubleshooting.

5 Click Using Windows 98 troubleshooters.

The basic guidelines for using troubleshooters are displayed in the right pane.

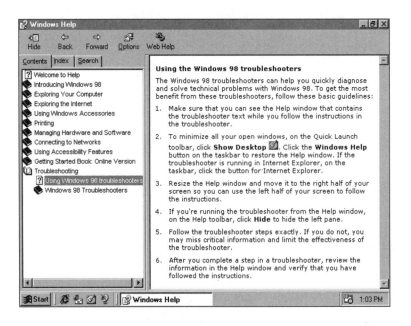

6 Read the basic guidelines for using troubleshooters, and then on the Contents menu, click Windows 98 Troubleshooters.

A list of available troubleshooters is displayed.

7 Close the Windows Help window.

Run the Windows 98 Print Troubleshooter

In this exercise, you use the Print Troubleshooter to help you diagnose and fix the problem with your printer. Notice as you move through the troubleshooter that the information displayed on your screen is dependent on your answer to the previous question.

1 Click the Start button, and then click Help.

The Windows Help window opens.

2 Click the Contents tab.

3 To see all the topics on the Contents tab, click the Maximize button.

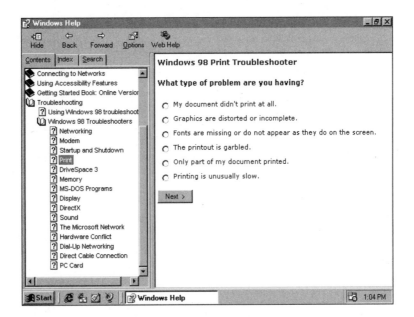

Maximize

4 Click Troubleshooting, click Windows 98 Troubleshooters, and then click Print.

The first question of the Print Troubleshooter and responses to the question are displayed in the right pane.

5 To hide the Contents tab, click the Hide button.

The Contents tab is hidden, and only the questions and responses are displayed.

6 Select the Print Out Is Garbled option, and then click Next.

The next question with responses is displayed in the right pane.

7

Using Windows 98 Tools

7 Select the I Am Printing To A Local Printer option, and then click Next.

The next question with responses is displayed in the right pane.

8 Select the I Don't Know option, and then click Next.

The troubleshooter displays a possible solution to the printing problem as well as steps to resolve the problem.

9 Try the solution, under the Did This Action Solve The Problem area, click Yes, and then click Next.

A message thanking you for using the Print Troubleshooter is displayed.

10 To see the Contents tab, click the Show button.

You can close the Windows Help window and continue with your work, or you can try another troubleshooter.

Using Windows 98 tools to diagnose and fix problems

Windows 98 includes tools that help you diagnose and solve computer problems. These tools are called *system tools*. Like fixing an auto or home repair problem, identifying the correct tool to use helps you fix your problem more efficiently. The following table briefly describes commonly used Windows 98 system tools.

System tool	Description
Disk Cleanup	Frees space on your hard disk by locating files that are no longer being used and suggesting what files can be safely deleted.
Disk Defragmenter	Rearranges files and unused space on your hard disk so that programs run faster.
ScanDisk	Checks your disk surface, files, and folders for errors.
System File Checker	Keeps track of critical files that enable your computer to run. The files can be restored if they are moved or damaged.

Imagine you have been working on your new computer for awhile. You realize that you are running out of disk space. One of your partners suggests that you run one of the system tools to see if you can clean up your hard disk and get more disk space. You decide to use the Disk Cleanup tool.

Use the Disk Cleanup tool to get more disk space

In this exercise, you run the Disk Cleanup tool to find and delete files that you don't need.

1 Click the Start button, point to Programs, point to Accessories, and then point to System Tools.

The System Tools menu is displayed.

2 On the System Tools menu, click Disk Cleanup.

The Select Drive dialog box appears.

❸ In the Drives box, be sure that drive C is displayed, and click OK.

The Disk Cleanup tool searches your hard disk to find files that you can delete. The Disk Cleanup For C dialog box appears. In the Disk Cleanup For C dialog box, a list of files to delete is displayed. The list includes four folders: Temporary Internet Files, Downloaded Program Files, Recycle Bin, and Temporary Files. The Temporary Internet Files folder includes the text, pictures, sound, video, and any other files included as a part of a Web page. This folder can grow quickly, and you should delete the contents to make room for new pages. Deleting the contents of the Temporary Internet Files folder does not delete a subscription or a link on your Favorites menu. The Downloaded Programs Files folder includes any programs you have downloaded from the Web. You should delete the programs you have installed on your computer to make room for more programs. Deleting the contents of this folder does not delete the program if you have installed it. If there are files located in the Temporary Internet Files folder and the Downloaded Program Files folder, the check box will be selected automatically.

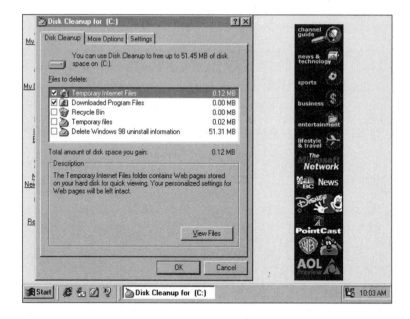

❹ If there is a number to the right of the Recycle Bin folder, then select the Recycle Bin check box.

The files in the Recycle Bin will be deleted. The Recycle Bin holds the files that you delete from your folders. The number to the right of the Recycle Bin folder shows how much disk space the files take up.

5 If there is a number to the right of the Temporary Files folder, then select the Temporary Files check box.

The files in the Temp folder will be deleted. The Temp folder is the folder that holds temporary files. When you open a document or a program, Windows 98 makes a temporary copy of the document or program and stores it in the Temp folder. When you close the document or program the temporary copy is deleted. However, the temporary copy might not be deleted. If it isn't deleted, it will remain in the Temp folder until you delete it.

6 Click OK.

A message confirming the deletion of the files is displayed.

7 Click Yes.

The Disk Cleanup tool deletes the files.

Periodically Backing Up Important Files and Folders

In the past, your firm relied on each worker to copy important files to floppy disks and store the floppy disks in a safe place. Unfortunately, it seemed that whenever a computer stopped working, the most crucial files were not safely copied. To correct this problem, you decide to implement a regular backup procedure using the Microsoft Backup program and a network drive.

You can back up files from your hard disk to any data storage device including a hard drive, tape drive, floppy disks, JAZ and ZIP drives, or even a folder specifically for backups on a network. The important consideration is that if your computer hard disk fails for any reason, irreplaceable files and data are not lost.

Backup hardware, such as a tape drive, often comes with its own backup program. However, if you do not have a backup program, you can install Microsoft Backup from the Windows 98 CD-ROM. The Backup program includes wizards to assist you with both backing up your files and with restoring files from a backup when the originals are lost or damaged.

Install the Microsoft Backup program

Before using Microsoft Backup, you first need to install it. In this exercise, you install Microsoft Backup.

1 Insert the Windows 98 CD-ROM in your CD-ROM drive.

2 Click the Start button, point to Settings, and then click Control Panel.

The Control Panel window opens.

3 Click the Add/Remove Programs icon.

The Add/Remove Programs Properties dialog box appears.

4 Click the Windows Setup tab.

The setup program checks for installed Windows 98 programs, and then a list of available programs is displayed.

5 In the Components list, click System Tools, and then click Details.

The System Tools dialog box appears.

6 In the System Tools Components list, select the Backup check box, and click OK.

The Add/Remove Programs Properties dialog box appears.

7 Click OK.

The setup program copies the files for the Backup program from the CD-ROM to the hard disk. A message prompting you to restart your computer so that changes to system files can be made is displayed.

8 Click Yes.

Your computer restarts, and the Backup option is added to the System Tools menu. When Windows 98 opens, the Control Panel window is open.

9 Close the Control Panel window.

Using Microsoft Backup

When you use Microsoft Backup, the Backup Wizard will appear and walk you through the process of backing up your files. You have several options when you use Microsoft Backup. For example, you can back up selected files, your entire hard disk, or just files and folders that were added or changed since your last backup. You can also select where and when to back up the files. However, before you schedule a backup, you must save the *backup job*. A backup job includes all the information you have entered, such as where to back up, the backup type, the backup device, and when to back up.

For the following exercise, imagine that you and your partners have decided that the computers should be backed up every Friday. Before a memo is sent out to the employees, you decide to test the Backup program but you don't want to back up to the network yet. You select a few files and back them up to a floppy disk.

tip
The steps on the following page can be used if you are backing up to a different source.

Using Windows 98 Tools

Back up selected files

In this exercise, you use the Backup program to back up one of your client folders to a floppy disk.

For a demonstration of how to use the backup program, in the AVIFiles folder on the Microsoft Windows 98 Step by Step CD-ROM, double-click the page180 icon.

① Insert a floppy disk in your floppy drive.

② Click the Start button, point to Programs, point to Accessories, and then point to System Tools.

The System Tools menu is displayed.

③ On the System Tools menu, click Backup.

The Backup program starts, and the Microsoft Backup dialog box appears, prompting you to create a new backup job, open an existing job, or restore backed up files.

If you don't have the backup hardware, such as a ZIP drive or tape drive, a message stating that the computer couldn't find the backup hardware is displayed. Click No when asked if you want to add new hardware.

![Screenshot of the Microsoft Backup dialog box showing the "Welcome to Microsoft Backup!" window with options to Create a new backup job, Open an existing backup job, or Restore backed up files.]

④ Click Create A New Backup Job option, and click OK.

The Backup Wizard dialog box appears. You can back up your entire hard disk, or you can select certain files to back up.

5 Click Back Up Selected Files, Folders And Drives, and then click Next.

You are now asked to select the check box next to the items you want to back up.

6 In the What To Backup pane, click the plus sign next to the drive C icon.

A list of folders on your hard disk is displayed.

7 Click the plus sign next to the Windows 98 SBS Practice Files folder.

A list of folders in the Windows 98 SBS Practice Files folder is displayed.

8 Click the plus sign next to the Correspondence folder.

Two folders are displayed.

9 Select the Duffy Stuff check box, and then click Next.

You are asked if you want to back up all selected files or files that have been added or changed since your last backup.

10 Click All Selected Files, and then click Next.

You are asked where to back up the files.

11 Click the folder icon next to C:\MyBackup.qic.

The Where To Back Up dialog box appears.

12 Click the Look In down arrow, click 3½ Floppy (A:), and then click Open.

The Where To Back Up The Files dialog box appears.

13 Click Next.

The How To Back Up dialog box appears.

14 Click Next.

You are asked to give the backup a name.

15 In the Type A Name For This Backup Job box type **Duffy Backup**, and then click Start.

The backup Progress dialog box appears, and the files you have selected are backed up to the floppy disk.

16 Click OK when a message informing you that the backup is complete is displayed.

17 Close all open windows.

Finish the lesson

1. To continue to the next lesson, close all open windows.

2. If you are finished using your computer for now, click the Start button, and then click Shut Down.

   The Shut Down Windows dialog box appears.

3. Select the Shut Down option, and click OK.

   The Windows 98 logo appears as the computer shuts down.

Lesson 7 Quick Reference

To	Do this
Connect to Windows Update	Click Start. Click Windows Update.
Run the Update Wizard	Connect to Windows Update. On the Windows Update home page, click Update Wizard. Follow the steps in the wizard.
Run a Windows 98 troubleshooter	Click Start. Click Help. Click the Contents tab. Click Windows 98 Troubleshooters. Click Troubleshooters. Click the appropriate troubleshooter. Answer troubleshooter diagnostic questions, and then follow the steps suggested to fix the problem.
Run Disk Cleanup	Click Start, point to Programs, point to Accessories, and then click Disk Cleanup. Select the drive you want to clean. Select each check box next to the folders if there are numbers to the right of the Temporary Internet Files, Downloaded Program Files, Recycle Bin, or Temporary Files folders. Click OK. Click Yes.
Install Microsoft Backup	Insert the Windows 98 CD-ROM in your CD-ROM drive. Click Start. Click Control Panel. Click Add/Remove Programs. Click the Windows Setup tab. Click System Tools. Click Details. Select Backup. Click OK. Click OK. Click Yes.
Start Microsoft Backup	Click Start, point to Programs, point to Accessories, point to System Tools, and then click Backup.

Lesson 7 Quick Reference

To	Do this	Button
Run the Backup Wizard	In the Microsoft Backup window, click the Backup Wizard button.	

PART

3

Review & Practice

ESTIMATED
TIME
20 min.

You will review and practice how to:

✔ *Schedule system tune-ups for the most convenient time of day.*

✔ *Change power management and accessibility settings to suit your needs.*

✔ *Connect to the Windows Update Web site and use the technical support line to answer questions about Windows 98.*

✔ *Back up your files and folders.*

Review & Practice

Before you move on to Part 4, which covers adding new hardware and software to your computer, you can practice the skills you learned in Part 3 by working through this Review & Practice section. You will reschedule tune-ups, change the power management settings, check to see if there are any updated Windows 98 files, and back up your folders and files.

Scenario

Your partner learned how to create and save files, browse the Web for information, and send messages to clients. He even copied a few programs from the Web. Now he'd like to learn how to make his computer run as efficiently as possible. He also feels frustrated with his tendency to press the CAPS LOCK key accidentally while he is typing. Considering you to be the most knowledgeable about Windows 98 at the firm, he approaches you about improving his computer's performance.

Step 1:   Change Settings to Improve Your Computer's Performance

The first performance enhancement you show your partner is how to use the
Maintenance Wizard to change the schedule for regular system maintenance.
You also show him how to save electricity or battery power by changing the
power management settings. Finally, you show him how to turn on ToggleKeys
so that he will be alerted when he presses the CAPS LOCK key.

1   Use the Maintenance Wizard to reschedule tune-ups to evenings from 8:00
P.M. to 11:00 P.M.

2   Open the Power Management Properties dialog box, and then change the
Turn Off Monitor option to after 4 hours.

3   Open the Accessibility Properties dialog box (Accessibility Options in the
Control Panel), and then turn on the ToggleKeys feature.

For more information about	See
Using the Maintenance Wizard to schedule regular system tune-ups	Lesson 6
Changing power management settings to save electricity or battery power	Lesson 6
Changing accessibility settings	Lesson 6

**Step 2:   Connect to Windows Update for Technical
Support and Windows 98 Upgrades**

To ensure that your partner always has the most current technical information
and software to support the hardware he buys, you show him how to connect to
the Windows Update Web site. You then demonstrate how to find an article by
searching for technical support on backing up files.

1   Connect to the Windows Update Web site.

2   Search for technical support documents on "backup."

3   View the article on using Backup to back up your files.

For more information about	See
Connecting to the Windows Update Web site	Lesson 7
Using Windows Update the technical support link	Lesson 7

Step 3:   **Back Up Important Folders and Files**

After reading the technical support documentation on backing up a hard disk, your partner decides he should learn how to back up his most important files and folders. You open the Microsoft Backup program and demonstrate by backing up the Client Logos folder to a floppy disk.

❶   Start Microsoft Backup, and then create a new backup job.

❷   Select the Client Logos folder in your Windows 98 Practice folder to back up, and then select the floppy disk drive as the destination for the backup file.

❸   Back up the Client Logos folder to a floppy disk.

For more information about	See
Installing and starting Microsoft Backup	Lesson 7
Selecting files and folders to back up	Lesson 7
Selecting a backup destination	Lesson 7

Finish the Review & Practice

❶   To continue to the next lesson, close any open windows or programs.

❷   Return the power management and accessibility settings to your preferred settings.

❸   If you are finished using your computer for now, click the Start button, and then click Shut Down.

❹   Select the Shut Down option, and click OK. The Windows 98 logo appears as the computer shuts down.

PART 4

Taking Your Computer to the Next Level

8

Adding New Hardware

ESTIMATED TIME 40 min.

In this lesson you will learn how to:

✔ *Attach hardware that is Plug and Play ready.*

✔ *Connect and use hardware that is USB ready.*

✔ *Use the DVD Player program to play DVD discs.*

✔ *Connect and use two monitors at a time.*

Now your firm has both the resources and the business needed to invest in new hardware. You want to take advantage of the new hardware technology. Some of this technology is in the form of DVD and Universal Serial Buses (USB). You have read that this new hardware technology is very easy to install and use with Microsoft Windows 98. You have also read that you can connect more than one monitor to your computer. Now you can research a topic on the Web and write your report without having to switch between two open windows.

In this lesson, you will install Plug and Play hardware. You will learn how to use new technologies such as USB and DVD, which can considerably expand the capability and usefulness of your computer system. You will also attach a second monitor to your computer and display a program window on one monitor and another program window on the other monitor.

Using New Hardware to Expand the Capabilities of Your Computer

When you buy a computer, it comes with a mouse, a keyboard, and a monitor. It might also include a CD-ROM drive and a modem. Like many people, you might find that you need additional hardware beyond the basics to make the most of your computer. For example, you might want to add a printer, a scanner, or a set of speakers. At work, you might need an overhead projector, hardware to connect to a network, or a writing tablet. At home, you might want to attach a joystick or a video camera.

Each piece of hardware you add to your computer needs a *driver* to make it run. A driver is a program that tells the computer how to work with a particular piece of hardware. Windows 98 includes many drivers and can support the majority of computer equipment available.

What is Plug and Play?

Plug and Play is a set of computer specifications that makes the computer, the hardware you are adding, the drivers for the new hardware, and Windows 98 work together with little or no actions required by you. All you have to do is add the new hardware to your computer while it's turned off and then turn on your computer. When Windows 98 starts, it searches to see if there is any new hardware. When new hardware is found, Windows 98 installs the drivers for the new hardware.

Install a Plug and Play scanner

You have bought a new scanner that is Plug and Play ready. In this exercise, you install the scanner.

> **tip**
> While the exercise describes installing a Plug and Play scanner, you can use the steps for any Plug and Play device.

1 If your computer is on, click the Start button, and then click Shut Down.

The Shut Down Windows dialog box appears.

2 Select the Shut Down option, and click OK.

Windows 98 shuts down.

3 Turn your computer off.

④ Following the instructions provided by the hardware manufacturer, connect the cable from the scanner to the appropriate port on the back of your computer.

⑤ Turn on the scanner, and then turn on your computer.

The New Hardware Found dialog box appears. Windows 98 loads the drivers. You might be asked to put your Windows 98 CD-ROM in your CD-ROM drive.

What is USB?

When you bought your computer, you might have read or heard the term USB. USB stands for Universal Serial Bus and is a special type of port built into computers in recent years. The USB port is for your *peripheral hardware*. Peripheral hardware is hardware that can be easily removed or added to your computer. Examples of peripheral hardware include digital cameras, hand-held scanners, joysticks, keyboards, mice, videophones, and printers. All of your peripheral hardware that is USB ready will have the same type of connector that is used to plug into the USB port on the back of your computer. Having the same connector will make it easier for you to plug in the hardware. For example, your mouse and keyboard will have the same connector and you don't have to worry which port to plug them into. You can plug and unplug your peripheral hardware without having to turn off your computer.

Some computers might only have one USB port. If you have more than one USB ready peripheral, you might want to buy a USB hub to connect all your USB ready peripherals into the one USB port in the back of your computer. A USB hub is a little box that has four USB ports on one end and a plug on the other end to plug into your USB port on the back of the computer. When you plug in the hub, you can plug in all your USB peripherals. You can also daisy-chain hubs if you need more ports. For example, your firm purchased a computer that has one USB port in the back. Your firm also purchased a USB ready scanner, mouse, keyboard, digital camera, and printer. You plug the USB hub into the USB port on the back of your computer. You then plug in three of your USB ready peripherals and another USB hub. You can now plug in the last two peripherals and use them. The USB hub plugged into the other USB hub is a daisy-chain.

Plug and unplug hardware from a USB port

You bought two new pieces of USB ready hardware, but your computer only has one USB port and you don't have a USB hub. In this exercise, you practice plugging in and unplugging the new hardware.

1 Take the connector at the end of the cable connected to the digital camera, and then plug it into the USB port.

Windows 98 searches for the digital camera driver and installs it. You are now ready to use the camera.

2 Unplug the camera.

3 Take the connector at the end of the cable connected to the scanner, and then plug it into the USB port.

Windows 98 searches for the scanner driver and installs it. You are now ready to use the scanner.

What is DVD?

DVD was originally designed for home video use. However, since its development, a wide variety of potential uses have been discovered. Currently, DVD discs are used mostly to store music, movies, and computer games. DVD drives can be read-only or read-write. Read-only means you can only use the files already on the disc. However, you can't add new files to the DVD disc. Read-write means you can copy files, videos, and so on to the DVD disc just like you can to a floppy disk. If you have a DVD that is read-write, you can store a large amount of information on the DVD disc. For example, you created a video for one of your clients and you need to send it to them. You can create a DVD disc of the video and mail it to your client.

View a video on your DVD drive

In this exercise, you will put a DVD video disc in your DVD drive and view it.

Depending on the manufacturer of your DVD drive, the DVD Player command might be placed on the Programs menu or on another menu within the Programs menu.

1 You should have a DVD drive installed on your computer. Press the button on the front of the DVD drive.

The DVD disc tray opens.

2 Place the DVD video disc in the disc tray, and then press the button on the front of the DVD drive.

The disc tray closes.

3 Click the Start button, point to Programs, and then click DVD Player.

The DVD Player dialog box appears. You can use the dialog box to start your video, pause it, or stop it. You are now ready to watch the video.

Viewing Information on Two or More Monitors

You have learned how to run more than one program at the same time. You can even switch back and forth between programs, copying and moving information from one program to another. Imagine you are working on a proposal for a client. You are using the Web to research a topic. You find yourself switching between your word processor and your browser. You might find it considerably more convenient to have one monitor for each program.

Windows 98 allows you to connect more than one monitor to your computer. With an additional piece of hardware called a video card, you can connect an additional monitor. You can add eight video cards to connect up to eight monitors.

Connect an additional monitor

In this exercise, you walk through the steps of attaching an additional monitor to your computer.

1 Click the Start button, and then click Shut Down.

The Shut Down Windows dialog box appears.

2 Select the Shut Down option, and click OK.

All windows are closed, and the computer shuts down.

3 Following the instructions provided by the video card manufacturer, remove the cover from your computer, and then install the video card without removing the current video card.

The video card supplies the additional port, or plug, you need for the second monitor.

4 Following the instructions provided by the video card manufacturer, attach the new monitor to the video card.

5 Turn on both monitors, and then turn on your computer.

The New Hardware Found dialog box appears, and Windows 98 installs the drivers. Your computer restarts. You might see the Plug and Play Wizard when Windows 98 starts. If you do see the wizard, click Next to accept the default settings. On the second monitor, a message saying that the display adapter was successfully initialized is displayed.

tip

If the second monitor stays black after Windows 98 has started, right-click your Desktop, and click Properties on the shortcut menu. Click the Settings tab, and then click the monitor 2 icon. Click Yes when prompted to enable the monitor, and click OK.

Changing the primary monitor

When you install multiple monitors, one monitor is designated as the *primary monitor*. The primary monitor is the one that displays the items on your Desktop. If the monitor you intend to use the most is not the primary monitor, you can change your monitors so the secondary monitor becomes the primary monitor. For example, you installed the second video card and plugged in your monitors. When you started Windows, you realized the monitor you wanted to be the primary is actually the secondary. You can change the monitors with very little effort.

Change your primary monitor

In this exercise, you switch the primary and secondary monitors.

1 Click the Start button, and then click Shut Down.

The Shut Down Windows dialog box appears.

2 Select the Shut Down option, and click OK.

All windows are closed, and the computer shuts down.

3 Unplug both monitors, and then reattach the monitors by plugging them into the opposite port.

The primary monitor will be attached to the original monitor port. The secondary monitor will be attached to the new video card.

Arranging multiple monitors

You have arranged your monitors on the desk side by side. The primary monitor is directly in front of you and the secondary monitor is to the left. Yet for some reason when you drag your mouse to the left, the mouse pointer doesn't appear on the secondary monitor. The Display Properties Settings tab includes an option that determines how you move items from one monitor to another. For example, if you're using two monitors and you want to move items from one monitor to the other by dragging left and right, position the monitor icons in the Settings tab side by side. To move items between monitors by dragging up and down, position the icons one above the other.

Arrange multiple monitors to reflect the physical arrangement

In this exercise, you arrange the monitors on the Settings tab to reflect how your monitors are physically arranged on your desk.

1 Be sure that more than one monitor is attached to your computer. Right-click the Desktop.

A shortcut menu is displayed.

2 On the shortcut menu, click Properties.

The Display Properties dialog box appears.

3 Click the Settings tab.

The Settings tab displays an icon representing each monitor attached to your computer. Your primary monitor is designated with the number 1 in the middle of the screen. The secondary monitor has the number 2 in the middle of the screen.

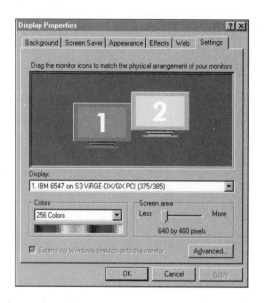

④ Drag the monitor icon for your secondary monitor to the position that represents the physical arrangement of your monitors, and then release the mouse button.

⑤ Right-click the monitor with the number 1 displayed.

A shortcut menu is displayed.

⑥ Click Identify.

A large number 1 appears on the screen of your primary monitor for a few seconds.

Move an open window from one monitor to the other

With multiple monitors installed and comfortably arranged, you are ready to run two programs side by side. In this exercise, you start Outlook Express and WordPad. You then move the WordPad window to your secondary monitor.

Launch Outlook Express

1. Be sure that you have more than one monitor attached to your computer. On the taskbar, click the Launch Outlook Express button.

   The Outlook Express window opens.

2. Click the Start button, point to Programs, and then point to Accessories.

   The Accessories menu is displayed.

3. On the Accessories menu, click WordPad.

   The WordPad window opens.

4. Drag the WordPad window from the primary monitor to the secondary monitor, and then release the mouse button when the outline of the WordPad window appears on your secondary monitor.

Copying data from one monitor to another

You copy information from a program window displayed on one monitor to a program window displayed on a second monitor the same way you copy information between program windows displayed on the same monitor. Using two monitors to copy information is easier since you can see both windows at once.

Copy data from one monitor to another

In this exercise, you open a file in WordPad and then copy text from the WordPad window in the secondary monitor into a New Message window in Outlook Express on the primary monitor.

1 Be sure that you have two monitors attached to your computer and you have WordPad running with the program window displayed on your secondary monitor. You have Outlook Express displayed on your primary monitor.

The Outlook Express window opens.

2 Click the My Computer icon, click the drive C icon, and then click the Windows 98 SBS Practice folder.

The Windows 98 SBS Practice folder opens.

3 Click the Market Plans folder.

The Market Plans window opens.

4 Click the MightyFlighty Plan file.

The MightyFlighty Plan file opens in a new WordPad window on the secondary monitor.

5 Highlight the contents of the MightyFlighty Plan by moving the mouse pointer to the beginning of the document, holding down the left mouse button and dragging the pointer down until all the text is highlighted.

6 On the Standard toolbar, click the Copy button.

The text of the MightyFlighty Plan file is copied to the Clipboard.

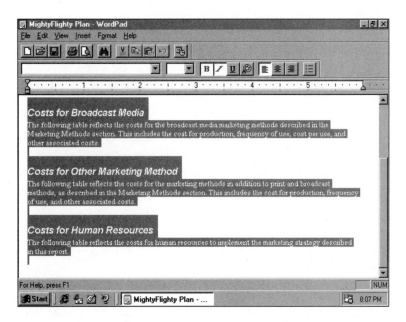

Compose Message

❼ In the Outlook Express window, click the Compose Message button.

A New Message window opens on the primary monitor.

❽ In the New Message window, click in the message pane, and then click the Paste button.

A copy of the MightyFlighty Plan text appears in the message pane.

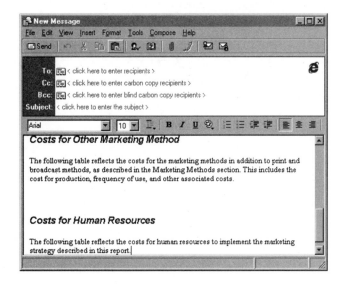

9 Close the New Message window and the Outlook Express window.

A message asking if you want to save the changes is displayed.

10 Click No.

11 Close the WordPad window.

A message asking if you want to save the changes is displayed.

12 Click No.

13 Close the Outlook Express window.

14 Close the Market Plans window.

One Step Further — Changing the Resolution of Your Second Monitor

You can change the resolution on your monitor so you can see more information. When you have two monitors, you can change the resolution on either or both of your monitors. For example, you decided you needed a larger monitor so your firm bought you a new 21-inch monitor. You attached the new monitor to your computer. When you started Windows 98, you opened two program windows and moved one of the program windows to the 21-inch monitor. You noticed that the text and buttons were very large, and you had to use the scroll bars to see your entire document. The program window on the other monitor is fine. You just want to change the display on the 21-inch monitor.

Change the resolution of your secondary monitor

1 Right-click a blank area on the Desktop.

A shortcut menu is displayed.

2 Click Properties.

The Display Properties dialog box appears.

3 Click the Settings tab.

Active monitor

Screen area
indicator

④ Click the monitor with the number 2 displayed on it.

⑤ Move the mouse pointer over the screen area indicator.

⑥ Drag the indicator to the right until 800 by 600 pixels is displayed, and then release the mouse button.

⑦ Click OK.

A message informing you that Windows will resize your Desktop is displayed.

⑧ Click OK.

Your screen will turn black for a few moments, and then the contents of the Desktop reappear. A message informing you that you are about to change your Desktop size and asking you if you want to keep the settings is displayed.

⑨ Click Yes.

Your resolution is changed, and your Desktop icons are smaller. If you want to return to your previous resolution, then follow the steps again and move the screen area indicator back to the far left.

Finish the lesson

① To continue to the next lesson, close any open windows.

② If you would like to return to a single monitor, turn off your computer, un-plug the secondary monitor, and then remove the second video card.

③ If you are finished using your computer for now, click the Start button, and then click Shut Down.

The Shut Down Windows dialog box appears.

4   Select the Shut Down option, and click OK.

The Windows 98 logo appears as the computer shuts down.

Lesson 8 Quick Reference

To	Do this
Install Plug and Play hardware	Turn off your computer. Attach the new hardware following the manufacturer's instructions. Turn your computer on.
Install hardware with a USB plug	Plug the USB hardware into the USB port on the back of your computer.
Start DVD Player	Your computer must have a DVD drive. Click the Start button, point to Programs, click Accessories, point to Entertainment, and then click DVD Player.
Attach a second monitor to your computer	Turn off your computer. Install a video card and the monitor following the manufacturer's instructions. Turn on the computer.
Change the primary and secondary monitors	Turn off your computer. Unplug the primary and secondary monitors. Switch the plugs, and then reattach them to your computer. Turn your computer on.
Arrange the mouse movement on multiple monitors	Right-click the Desktop, and then click Display Properties. Click the Settings tab. Arrange the icons to represent the physical arrangement of your monitors.
Move an open window from one monitor to the other	Start a program. Move the mouse pointer to the title bar of the program window. Drag the program window from the primary monitor to the secondary monitor. Release the mouse button.
Copy data from a program displayed on one monitor to another program displayed in the other monitor	Open a program. Move the program window to the secondary monitor. Open another program. Select the data to copy, and then click the Copy button. Click in the window of the other program, and then click the Paste button.
Change the size of the display in the second monitor	Right-click a blank area on the Desktop, and then click Properties. Click the Settings tab. Click the monitor with the number 2. Drag the screen area indicator to the right. Click OK. Click OK. Click Yes.

9

Combining Your Computer with a Television

ESTIMATED TIME
40 min.

In this lesson you will learn how to:

✔ *Set up your computer so it functions like a television.*

✔ *Use your computer to find television programs.*

✔ *Watch a television program on your computer.*

✔ *Search for a television program by name and by category.*

✔ *View Web pages about a television program.*

As employees of a public relations firm, you and your partners need almost constant access to cable and network television to keep informed of current news and market conditions. In the past, you had to look in the newspaper for the times of particular programs and then go to one of your conference rooms to watch the program on the television. With Microsoft Windows 98, you can search the Web TV program on your computer for a television program and then watch it on your computer.

In this lesson, you will learn how you can use your computer as a television using Windows 98 and a TV tuner card. You will explore Web TV and learn how to view channel listings and search for television programs by name and category. You will also learn how to view the television programs on your computer.

Interacting with Web TV and Your Computer

Windows 98 supports the technology that combines a computer and a television. To make your computer receive a television signal, you need to install a TV tuner card. With a tuner card your computer can receive and display television broadcasts on the monitor, using a standard television cable connection. The television cable is connected to your tuner card in the back of your computer. After you install the tuner card, you need to install Web TV from the Windows 98 CD-ROM. You then use the G-Guide™ program to download the television program listings from your cable provider.

You and your partners would like to use this technology on your computers in the office. After you install Web TV, you install the G-Guide™ program listing.

Install the Web TV for Windows program

1 Place the Windows 98 CD-ROM in your CD-ROM drive.

2 Click the Start button, point to Settings, and then click Control Panel.

The Control Panel window opens.

3 Click the Add/Remove Programs icon.

The Add/Remove Programs Properties dialog box appears.

4 Click the Windows Setup tab.

The Windows Setup program searches for installed Windows 98 programs.

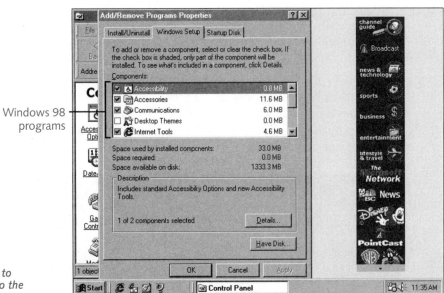

Windows 98 programs

You must be set up to connect to the Internet to complete this exercise.

Launch Web TV For Windows

5 Select the Web TV For Windows check box, and click OK.

The Windows Setup program copies the files from the CD-ROM to your hard disk and adds the Launch Web TV For Windows button to the Quick Launch toolbar. A message prompting you to restart your computer is displayed.

6 Click Yes.

Windows 98 closes and your computer restarts. When Windows 98 starts, the Building Driver Database dialog box appears. Next the New Hardware Found dialog box appears. After the Web TV software is installed, the software will find and configure your tuner card. This process might have you restart your computer more than once, depending on the type of TV tuner card you have.

7 Close the Control Panel window.

Your Computer with a TV   9

Start Web TV for the first time

 On the Quick Launch toolbar, click the Launch Web TV For Windows button.

The Web TV for Windows program starts. Based on your reception or cable subscription, Web TV must scan the channels so it can identify which television stations to load on your computer. If the Launch Web TV For Windows button is not visible on the Quick Launch toolbar, drag the toolbar divider to the right.

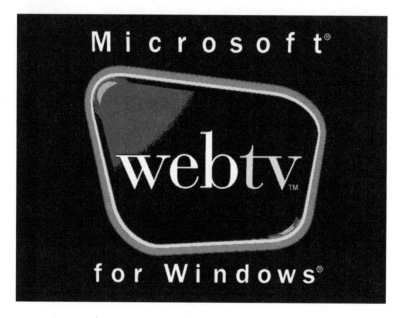

2 Click Start Scan.

Web TV begins to scan for channels you can receive. This might take a few minutes.

3 When the scan is complete, type your zip code and then click Next.

The Get TV Listings option appears.

4 Click the G-Guide™ link.

The browser window opens and the TV program listings page appears.

5 Click the New Site Link.

The Brodcast Region page appears and a list of breadcast regions offered by your cable company is displayed.

6 Click the your broadcast region and then click save.

The Get Program Listings page appears.

❼   Click the Get Listings link.

 The program listings are downloaded to your computer. This might take a few minutes.

❽   When the download is completed close your browser window.

❾   Click Finish.

 The Program Guide will load. This might take a few minutes.

Using Web TV to find television programs

You can use the Program Guide in Web TV to find a television program. Like television listings in your local newspaper, TV programming is presented in a grid that displays each channel down the left side and the time of day across the top. You can use the scroll bars or the menu options to find a television program. With the Program Guide, you can quickly find a television program on your computer and then watch it. You can get updates for your Program Guide from the Web whenever you want. The timeslots for television programs that are currently playing are green while the timeslots for television programs that aren't playing are blue. When you click a program, you will see the information about the program in the description area on the right side of the Program Guide. You will also see icons under the title of the program. The following table gives a description of the icons you might see.

Icon	What it means
⏰	You have set a reminder. You can set reminders so you won't miss a television program you want to watch.
🎧	Stereo is available.
💬	Closed caption is available.
↻	The program is a rerun.

You can quickly find a program using the Search function. You can search by category, channel, title, actor, actress, or critic rating. Web TV searches the entire Program Guide and returns a list of shows meeting your criteria. You can then narrow the search to just a single day. You can also sort the results by time or title. When the list of shows is displayed, the show listed in the first row will appear in the display panel in the upper-right corner of the description area.

Your Computer with a TV 9

You can also set a reminder for programs that you want to watch. For example, you and one of your clients held a press conference about a new toy that is being released to stores. You want to be reminded when the news on channel 4 is starting so you can watch the press conference. When the television program starts, a dialog box reminding you that the television program is about to begin will appear on your Desktop, even if you are not watching TV on your computer at the time. However, your computer must be on for the reminder to appear.

Use the Program Guide to view program listings

In this exercise, you will browse your local listings in the Program Guide.

 Be sure that Web TV is open. Press F10, and then click the Guide button.
The Program Guide window opens.

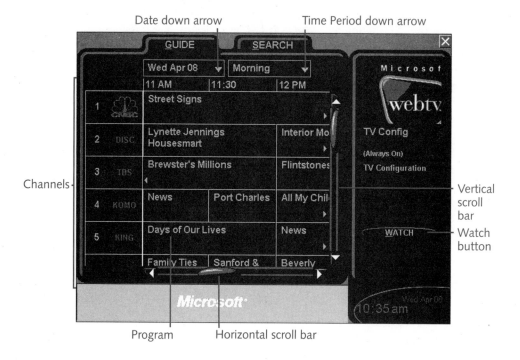

 Click the Time Period down arrow, and then click Evening.
The Program Guide displays programs for the evening hours, starting at 5:00 P.M.

Different time periods

GUIDE	SEARCH			X

Wed Apr 08 ▼   Evening ▼

Microsoft
webtv
for Windows'

		5 PM	5:30	Early AM	12 AM to 06 AM
3	TBS	Miami Heat at New		Morning	06 AM to 12 PM
				Afternoon	12 PM to 05 PM
				Now	
4	KOMO	News		Evening	05 PM to 09 PM
				Night	09 PM to 12 AM

News
ews & Talk, News
5:00 PM - 6:00 PM
NR(Not Rated)

5	KING	News	NBC News
6	KONG	Emergency!	Adam-12
7	KIRO	News	CBS News
		Dear God	Jingle All the Way

REMIND

OTHER TIMES

98002 - 980052   Bellevue - Seattle

Wed Apr 08
2 37 pm

❸ Click the Day And Date down arrow, and then click tomorrow's date.

The Program Guide displays programs for tomorrow evening.

❹ Drag the horizontal scroll box to the left.

The Program Guide displays programs for tomorrow at 4:30 P.M. Each time you move the scroll box, the Program Guide adjusts the time range displayed.

❺ Click the vertical scroll bar down arrow.

The Program Guide displays additional channels. Each time you click the vertical scroll bar arrow, the Program Guide changes the channels displayed.

❻ In the Program Guide window, click a program.

A blue box appears around the program timeslot, and the content information about the program appears on the right side of the Web TV window.

Watch a television program on your computer

1 Be sure that Web TV is open. Press F10, and then click the Guide button.

The Program Guide window opens. The Guide tab is the default tab and appears every time you start Web TV.

2 Click the time period down arrow and click Now.

The Program Guide displays shows that can be currently viewed. Current playing programs have a green background.

3 In the Program Guide window, click a program that is playing now.

The television program is displayed in the upper-right corner of the Program Guide window.

4 Click Watch.

A full screen view of the television program is displayed.

5 Press F10 when you are finished, and then click the Close button.

Web TV closes. If you want to watch another television program, click the Guide button, and then choose another program.

Search for a particular television program.

In this exercise, you use the Search feature to find the programs you need to watch.

 Be sure that Web TV is open. Click the Search tab.

The Search window opens. You will search for a television program.

 In the Search box, type **News**

The Search feature will look at the program name, content information, and list of actors and actresses. You could type a word such as "comedy" or "Luke" to produce a television program you are interested in.

 Click the Search button.

Web TV searches the Program Guide for listings containing the word "News" and then displays the results.

Search for a television program by category

In this exercise, you search for listings in the Program Guide based on program category.

❶ Be sure that Web TV is open. Click the Search tab.

The Search window opens. You will search for a news program.

❷ Under Categories, click News And Talk.

A list of news and talk shows is displayed in the search results.

❸ Click the Day menu down arrow, and then click today's date.

Only news and talk shows being shown today are displayed in the search results.

❹ Click the Sort menu down arrow, and then select Sort By Title.

The search results are displayed in alphabetical order by title.

Set a reminder for a program you want to watch

In this exercise, you set a reminder for a News and Talk television program. You set the reminder alert to appear only once 10 minutes before the show is about to start.

❶ Be sure that the Program Guide window is open and the Guide tab is active.

❷ Click a future television program listing.

Since you are practicing setting reminders, you might want to select a program that will start within the next half hour so that you can see the reminder appear on your computer soon.

❸ Click the Remind button.

The Remind dialog box appears.

❹ Select the Once option.

You can set a reminder to alert you only once or every time the television program is run either daily or weekly.

❺ Click the Minutes down arrow, and then click 10.

You can choose when you want the reminder to appear.

❻ Click OK.

In the Description box, a reminder is set for the program. Ten minutes before the program starts, an alert dialog box will appear on your computer.

❼ Click the Search tab and then scroll down in the Categories list and click My Reminders.

A list of pending reminders is displayed. After the program time passes, the reminder will be removed from the list of My Reminders.

Using the Web to Learn More About Your Favorite Show

You can combine watching a television program with getting information from the Web. When you choose a television program to watch, you can learn more about the actors, the topic being discussed, or the product being advertised. The title of the television program is a link to the Web. When you click the link, your browser window opens and a list of links are displayed. For example, you are watching a program and you know that the content would be of interest to one of your clients. You can get more information for your client by clicking the title of the television program and viewing the links that are displayed.

Many television programs are already supported by Web pages on the Internet. Production companies and television networks create some of these pages while fans of the show generate others.

View Web pages about a television program

In this exercise, you use Web TV to find links to Web pages about a television program.

Launch Web TV For Windows

1 On the taskbar, click the Launch Web TV For Windows button.

The Web TV window opens and hides the taskbar.

2 Click the Search tab.

The Search window opens.

3 In the search box, type **Headline News** and then click Search.

Web TV searches the Program Guide for listings containing the phrase "Headline News" and displays the results.

4 Click the first listing for Headline News.

The content information about the listing appears on the right.

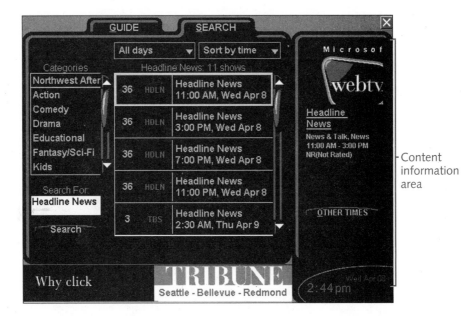

5 In the content information area, click the Headline News link.

The browser window opens and connects to an Internet search engine. A list of links about the program Headline News is displayed.

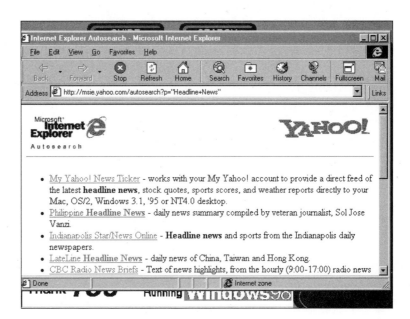

⑥ Click the first link for Headline News. Read the information. When you are finished, close the browser window.

Close

Exit Web TV

❶ Be sure that Web TV is open. Point to the top of your monitor.

The Web TV title bar appears. You can also press F10 to display the Web TV title bar.

❷ Click the Close button.

One Step Further Scheduling Your Program Guide Updates

Once you have setup Web TV and downloaded the G-Guide™ TV listings, you might want to change the time of day you receive updates. The default time for receiving updates in 1:00 A.M. Since your computer must be turned on to receive updates, this time may not be convenient for you. You can set a time for when you will have your computer on, but not running the Web TV program.

Schedule G-Guide™ TV Listing updates

In this exercise, you will change the time the G-Guide™ will be updated.

1   Be sure that Web TV is open.

2   Use your vertical scroll bar to scroll to the last channel listed.

3   Double-click TV Configuration.

The Web TV Welcome screen is displayed. You should hear an audio introduction to Web TV.

4   Click Go To.

The Go To screen is displayed.

5   Click Schedule Updates.

The Schedule Update screen is displayed.

6   Click on the first number and begin typing the time you wish to receive updates.

As you type the numbers, the selector moves to the next cell.

7   Click Go To and then click Configuration Complete.

8   Click Finish.

The Program Guide appears.

Finish the lesson

1   To continue to the next lesson, close any open windows.

2   If you are finished using your computer for now, click the Start button, and then click Shut Down.

The Shut Down Windows dialog box appears.

3   Select the Shut Down option, and click OK.

The Windows 98 logo appears as the computer shuts down.

4   Turn off your computer.

Lesson 9 Quick Reference

To	Do this	Button
Install the Web TV for Windows program	Insert the Windows 98 CD-ROM in your CD-ROM drive. Click the Start button, point to Settings, and then click Control Panel. Click the Add/Remove Programs icon. Click the Windows Setup tab. Select the Web TV For Windows check box, and click OK. Click Yes. Close the Control Panel window.	
Start Web TV for Windows for the first time	Click the Launch Web TV For Windows button. Click Start Scan. Type your ZIP code. Click Next. Click G-Guide™ link. Click the New Site link. Click the cable provider link. Click Download. Close the browser window. Click Finish.	
Use the Program Guide to view program listings for the following evening	Click the Launch Web TV For Windows button. Click the Guide tab. Click the Time Range down arrow, and then click Evening. Click the Day And Date down arrow, and then click tomorrow's date. Use the scroll bar to find the program you want to watch. Click the program.	
Watch a TV program on your computer	In the Program Guide window, click the program. In the content information area, click Watch.	
Search for a program by title using Web TV	Click the Search tab. In the search box, type the title. Click Search.	
Search for a program by category using Web TV	Click the Search tab. Under Categories, click the name of the category you are interested in.	
Display Internet Web pages about a particular television program	In the Program Guide window, click the program. In the content information pane, click the title of the television program link.	
Close Web TV	Point to the top of the monitor. On the title bar, click the Close button.	

Your Computer with a TV

9

10

Using Your Computer at Home

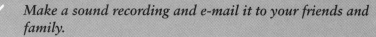

ESTIMATED
TIME
40 min.

In this lesson you will learn how to:

✔ *Set up an Internet connection and an Internet mail account.*

✔ *Connect to the Internet from your home using a modem.*

✔ *Watch video on your monitor.*

✔ *Make a sound recording and e-mail it to your friends and family.*

You might use a personal computer both at work and at home. When your company upgrades to Microsoft Windows 98, you decide to upgrade your home computer as well to make working from home as easy as possible. You also want to take advantage of the considerable new and enhanced features Windows 98 offers for home computer users. For example, connecting to an Internet Service Provider has never been easier. Also, you can use Windows 98 tools to improve the images, sound, and performance of games.

In this lesson, you will explore ways to make the most of your home computer. You will connect to the Internet using your modem and visit a Web site. You will learn about enhancements to game performance and attach game-related hardware, such as joysticks, to your computer. You will also explore Windows 98 multimedia programs that make it possible to view video and record sounds.

Connecting to the World Wide Web from Home Using Your Modem

After using the World Wide Web at work, you realize the tremendous information and recreational resources available. Every time you connect to the Web to do research for a client, you might feel tempted to look for topics of personal interest. For example, you might be interested in bike riding, traveling, or gardening. Now that you know how to use the browser window and search engines, you would like to go home and "surf" the Web on your own time.

Fortunately, you can connect to the Web with a local telephone call from almost anywhere. If you have a laptop computer, you can even use your cellular phone. All you need to connect to the Web is a modem that has a cellular phone connector for you to use with your cellular phone. To connect to the Web from home or with your laptop, you must establish an account with a local Internet Service Provider (ISP). You can use the Online Services menu in Windows 98 to select and sign up with one of the service providers. Alternatively, if you live in the United States, you can usually find listings in your area phone book under Internet Providers & Services.

Your ISP will supply you with information about setting up your account. With this information, you can run the Internet Connection Wizard to create a dial-up connection. The dial-up connection contains the settings your computer needs to connect to the Internet. The wizard prompts you for everything needed to use your modem to call, connect to, and log on to the ISP, exchange e-mail, and browse the World Wide Web. When you open Microsoft Outlook Express and the browser window, you will be prompted to log on, and then you can create, read, reply to, or send messages.

You have decided to sign up with a local ISP rather than a national online service. When you called the ISP, they provided you with connection settings such as your username, password, e-mail account information, and the name of the server you will connect to.

tip
Some Internet Service Providers will walk you through setting up an Internet connection when you sign up with them.

Set up your Internet connection

Before you begin this exercise, review the steps to see if you are missing any information, and then contact your ISP for more details if necessary.

In this exercise, you use the Internet Connection Wizard and the information from your ISP to create a dial-up connection. If you have completed Lesson 8, you can skip this exercise.

❶ Click the Start button, point to Programs, point to Internet Explorer, and then click Connection Wizard.

The Internet Connection Wizard dialog box appears.

❷ Click the I Have An Existing Internet Service Through A Local Area Network Or Internet Service Provider option, and then click Next.

❸ Click the Connect Using My Phone Line option, and then click Next.

The Connect Using My Local Area Network option can only be used if you are connected to a network, usually in a corporate setting.

❹ Click the Create A New Dial-Up Connection option, and then click Next.

❺ Type the phone number your modem dials to connect to your ISP's computer, and then click Next.

This is the number used to connect to the ISP computer, not the number you would use to call Technical Support or Sales.

Most ISP passwords are case-sensitive. The passwords can consist of any combination of uppercase and lowercase letters, and you must be careful to type the password the same way each time.

❻ Type your username and password, and then click Next.

Some ISPs allow you to select your own username and password while others will assign them to you. You are asked if you want to change the advanced settings of your dial-up connection.

❼ Click the No option, and then click Next.

Some ISPs require that you change the advanced settings for your computer. Your ISP will alert you if this is necessary and supply the additional information. If you select the Yes option, the wizard will prompt you through entering advanced settings information.

❽ Type a name for your dial-up connection, and then click Next.

You can type any name you want. The name is used to help you identify your dial-up connection. You are asked if you want to set up your Internet mail account.

❾ Click the No option, and then click Next.

The steps to set up your Internet mail account are located in the next exercise, "Set up your Internet mail account." You are asked if you want to set up your Internet news account.

❿ Click the No option, and then click Next.

You are asked if you want to set up your Internet directory service.

⓫ Click the No option, and then click Next.

If you select the Yes option, you can select an Internet directory service. If you do select this option, you will need additional information from your ISP to set up the Internet directory service. An Internet directory service functions like a telephone book for e-mail addresses.

⓬ Click Finish.

The Internet Connect Wizard dialog box closes.

Set up your Internet mail account

If you have completed Lesson 8, you can skip this exercise.

Launch Outlook Express

❶ On the Quick Launch toolbar, click the Launch Outlook Express button.

The Outlook Express window opens.

❷ On the Tools menu, click Accounts.

The Internet Accounts dialog box appears.

❸ Click the Add button, and then click Mail.

The Internet Connection Wizard dialog box appears.

❹ Type your name, and then click Next.

You are prompted to enter your e-mail address.

❺ Type your e-mail address, and then click Next.

This should be the same e-mail address that you set up with your ISP. You are asked for your e-mail server names.

Internet Connection Wizard

E-mail Server Names

My incoming mail server is a [POP3 ▼] server. Type the name of your incoming mail server.

Incoming mail (POP3 or IMAP) server:

[   ]

An SMTP server is the server that is used for your outgoing e-mail. Type the name of your SMTP server.

Outgoing mail (SMTP) server:

[   ]

[< Back] [Next >] [Cancel] [Help]

6 Type the POP3 server name that your ISP provided, and then press TAB.

The cursor moves to the Outgoing Mail Server box. POP3 stands for Post Office Protocol. It is an alternative e-mail protocol used to serve intermittent dial-up connections to the Internet. Your mail is held until you make a connection and request your e-mail.

7 Type the SMTP server name that your ISP provided, and then click Next.

SMTP stands for Simple Mail Transfer Protocol. SMTP allows messages to be sent from one computer to another computer even if the second computer has a different type of operating system.

8 Type your POP account name that your ISP provided, and then press TAB.

The cursor moves to the Password field.

9 Type your password, and then click Next.

This password is generally the same password you use in your dial-up connection.

10 Type a name for this account, and then click Next.

You can type any name you want. The name is used to help you easily identify your e-mail account.

11 Click the Connect Using My Phone Line option, and then click Next.

12 Click the Use An Existing Dial-Up Connection, and then click the name of the connection in the white box.

The connection name is the one you created when you set up your dial-up connection.

13 Click Next.

You have finished setting up your e-mail account.

14 Close the Internet Accounts dialog box.

Connecting to the Internet using your modem

Once you have set up your Internet connection, you can use your modem to connect to the Internet. You find that using the browser window on your computer at home is the same as using the browser window on your computer at work. You can use the same search engines and you can go to the same Web sites that you use at work. However, since you are at home you can now browse the Web for information that is of personal interest to you.

Connect to the Internet using your modem

1 Click the My Computer icon.

The My Computer window opens.

2 Click the Dial-Up Networking folder.

The Dial-Up Networking folder opens.

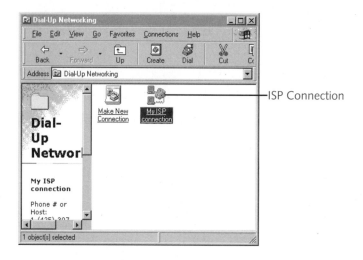

ISP Connection

3 Click the dial-up connection icon for your Internet account.

The Connect To dialog box appears.

4 In the Password box, type your password.

You can select the Save Password check box if you don't want to be prompted to type your password each time you use the dial-up connection. If you do select the check box, make sure you remember your password in case you wish to change it in the future.

5 Click the Connect button.

The modem dials your ISP. Then the dial-up connection connects to your ISP's server and logs in. When the connection is established, the Connection Established dialog box appears.

6 Click Close.

The Connection Established dialog box closes. Notice the Dial-Up icon on your taskbar to the left of the date. This indicates that you are connected to your ISP's computer.

7 Close the Dial-Up Networking window.

You are now ready to open your Internet browser window or check to see if you have received new messages.

Open your browser and search for Web pages about a particular topic

In this exercise, you open your browser window and then use a search engine to look for specific information on the Web.

If you are not connected to the Internet when you start this exercise, you will be prompted to log on to your ISP when you click the Launch Internet Explorer Browser button.

If Yahoo is not available, choose one of the other search engines.

1 Be sure that you are connected to your ISP. Open your Internet browser.

The browser window opens and displays your home page. The home page is the first Web page you see when you connect to the Internet or when you visit someone's Web site.

2 Click the Search button.

The Search pane appears on the left side of the browser window.

3 Click the Choose A Search Engine link, and then click Yahoo.

The Search pane displays the Yahoo search engine.

4 In the search box, type **plants+gardens**

The plus (+) symbol forces the search engine to look for Web pages that include both "plants" and "gardens."

5 In the Search pane, click the Search button.

A message warning you that you are about to send information over the Internet is displayed.

6 Click yes.

Yahoo searches for Web pages and articles containing both "plants" and "gardens."

7 Click the first link in the list of categories.

The Web page related to the link appears with an additional list of links.

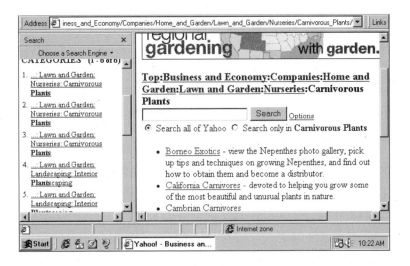

8 On the Search bar, click the Close button.

The Search pane closes and the Display pane expands to fill the browser window.

9 Browse through the links.

10 When you are finished browsing, close the browser window.

Exchanging e-mail using Outlook Express with a dial-up connection

You can exchange e-mail with friends, family, and business colleagues on the Internet from home using your dial-up connection and Outlook Express. Your ISP stores your new e-mail until you connect to the Internet. When you establish a connection and start Outlook Express, your outgoing mail is sent to your ISP, who forwards it to the recipients, and your incoming mail is moved to your hard disk.

Start Outlook Express with a dial-up connection

In this exercise, you open Outlook Express and send and receive e-mail.

If you are not connected when you start this exercise, you will be prompted to log on to your ISP when you click the Launch Outlook Express button.

1 Be sure that you are connected to your ISP. On the Quick Launch toolbar, click the Launch Outlook Express button.

The Outlook Express window opens. Outlook Express automatically sends outgoing mail and moves incoming mail to your Inbox.

2 Read your incoming mail.

If you compose and send any messages, they will be immediately forwarded to your ISP and sent to the recipients. When you have finished with your e-mail, close the Outlook Express window.

Launch Outlook Express

Disconnect from your ISP

You have finished both exchanging mail and browsing the Web. In this exercise, you disconnect from your ISP.

1 On the taskbar, double-click the Dial-Up icon.

The Connected dialog box appears.

2 Click Disconnect.

Your computer logs off the ISP account and then releases your dial-up connection.

Using Improved Game Performance Technology

Whether you have been playing computer games since the first version of Pong or have only recently discovered the game aisle at your local electronics store, computer games can consume a good portion of your recreational time.

For more information on performance enhancement, see Lesson 6, "Improving Speed, Efficiency, and Accessibility." For more information about new hardware, see Lesson 8, "Adding New Hardware."

Windows 98 incorporates many new technologies to improve and expand game performance. Overall computer performance enhancements, such as conversion to FAT32 and Windows 98 tune-ups, make games run faster and more smoothly. New hardware such as DVD and multiple monitors tremendously increase the options available to game designers for multiple players, imaging, and sound.

With USB technology, you can use new game controllers such as more sensitive joysticks, steering wheels, and drawing pads. For example, you can plug in a joystick for a helicopter game. When you want to switch to a driving game with a steering wheel, you can unplug the joystick from the USB port and plug in the steering wheel without having to turn off your computer.

In addition, Windows 98 supports multiple players. For example, if you have two USB ports or a USB hub, you can attach multiple joysticks to a single computer. Combined with multiple monitors, you can set up your one home computer to support a multi-player game for the entire household. See Lesson 8, "Adding New Hardware," for more information about multiple monitors.

Exploring New Multimedia Programs

Another enhancement to Windows 98 that intrigues you is the multimedia programs. With programs such as ActiveMovie Control or Sound Recorder you can watch video clips or record sounds. In addition, the World Wide Web has many sites devoted to free animation graphics, videos, and sounds that you can experience and then copy to your hard disk for personal use.

Run a video clip using ActiveMovie Control

In this exercise, you use ActiveMovie Control to open and run a video clip from the Windows 98 SBS Practice folder.

1 Click the My Computer icon, click the drive C icon, and then click the Windows 98 SBS Practice folder.

The Windows 98 SBS Practice folder opens.

2 Click the Elephants file.

The ActiveMovie Control program starts, opens the Elephants file, and runs the video clip. When the clip is complete, the ActiveMovie Control program closes.

Record and play a sound message

You must have a sound card, speakers, and a microphone to do this exercise.

In this exercise, you record, play, and save a birthday message. If your sound recorder is not installed, see Appendix B for steps to install the sound recorder.

1 Click the Start button, point to Programs, and then point to Accessories.

2 On the Accessories menu, point to Entertainment, and then click Sound Recorder.

The Sound Recorder program starts.

Progress bar

For a demonstration of how to record, play, and save a message, in the AVIFiles folder on the Microsoft Windows 98 Step by Step CD-ROM, double-click the page231 icon.

Rewind

Fast Forward   Play   Stop   Record

❸ Hold the microphone about an inch from your mouth, and then click the Record button.

The Sound Recorder program begins recording.

❹ Say **Happy Birthday!**

The Sound Recorder program records your voice.

❺ Click the Stop button.

The recording stops. You will now play the sound back to check for quality.

❻ Click the Play button.

Sound Recorder plays your recorded message.

❼ On the File menu, click Save.

The Save As dialog box appears.

❽ Click the Save In down arrow, and then click drive C.

The contents of drive C are displayed.

❾ Double-click the Windows 98 SBS Practice folder.

The contents of the Windows 98 SBS Practice folder are displayed.

Using Your Computer at Home   10

10 In the File Name box, type **Happy Birthday** and then click Save.

The sound file is saved to the Windows 98 SBS Practice folder as Happy Birthday.

11 Close the Sound Recorder window.

Attaching a file to an e-mail message

Sending files via e-mail is a great way to share information with your friends and family. You can send any type of file as an attachment including video, graphics, sound, or word processing. When a person receives a file attached to an e-mail, they can read, view, listen to, save, or print the file. For example, you have a family member who is having a birthday. You can attach a recorded birthday greeting to an e-mail message and then send the message.

important

Video and audio files can be very large. If you send large files over the Internet, it might take a long time to download the files and it might cause problems if the recipient has an ISP that charges by the hour.

Attach a sound to an e-mail message

In this exercise, you practice sending an e-mail message with an attached sound file.

Launch Out-look Express

Compose New Message

1 On the taskbar, click the Launch Outlook Express button.

The Outlook Express window opens.

2 Click the Compose New Message button.

The New Message window opens.

3 In the To field, type the e-mail address of the person you want to receive this e-mail.

4 In the Subject field, type **Happy Birthday!**

If the file you are attaching is a PC sound file, it might not play on a Macintosh computer or a computer with the Unix operating program installed.

Insert File

⑤ In the message pane, type a message.

When you send attachments, it is a good idea to explain the purpose and file type of the attachment. If the recipient is unfamiliar with computers, you might also want to explain how to open the file. For example, you might type "Just wanted to wish you a very happy 40th! The attached file is a sound recording. Just double-click it to hear the message."

⑥ Click the Insert File button.

The Insert Attachment dialog box appears.

⑦ Click the Look In down arrow, and then click drive C.

The contents of drive C are displayed.

⑧ Double-click the Windows 98 SBS Practice folder.

The contents of the Windows 98 SBS Practice folder are displayed.

⑨ Click the Happy Birthday 2 file, and then click Attach.

The Insert Attachment dialog box closes. An attachment pane appears at the bottom of the New Message window. The sound file appears in the attachment pane.

Using Your Computer at Home 10

Attached file

10 Click the Send button.

The message moves to the Outbox and from there it is sent to the recipient.

One Step Further
Create and Save a Unique Desktop for Each Member of Your Household

Sometimes more than one person uses the same computer. For example, at home you might have several members of your household who share a computer. User profiles make it possible for users to customize their Desktop colors and backgrounds, screen savers, commands on the Favorites and Start menus, and My Documents folder settings.

When you turn on a computer that is set up for multiple users, a dialog box appears, prompting you for a username and password. When you type in your username and password, Windows 98 sets up your personal settings. For example, you could change your Desktop colors to orange and purple while another person could use green and yellow. You could each create your own shortcuts and place them on the Start and Favorites menu or on the Desktop.

You can also protect your settings and documents from other users by using a password. Passwords are often a good idea in homes with children, shielding you from their notions of clever screen colors and shielding your children from your Active Desktop items, Favorites, and documents that you don't want them to open.

Create a user profile for yourself

In this exercise, you create your own user profile. The steps to create a user profile are the same if you need to create more than one user pro file.

If there is already one or more user profile, the User Settings dialog box appears. Click New User.

1 Click the Start button, point to Settings, and then click Control Panel.

The Control Panel window opens.

2 Click the Users icon.

The Enable Multi-User Wizard dialog box appears.

3 Type your name, and then click Next.

Each user profile will be identified by name. In your own household, for example, you might want to just use first names.

4 If you would like to use passwords, in the Password box, type a password, press TAB, and then type the password again.

You do not have to use passwords. They are a good idea, however, if you have children in the household and you would like to block them from either using or changing your Desktop settings or your Web favorites.

5 Click Next.

The Personal Items list is displayed. You can select one or more items you want to personalize. In this exercise, you will select all of the items.

6 Select the Desktop Folder And Documents Menu check box, select the Start Menu check box, select the Favorites Folder check box, select the Downloaded Web Pages check box, and then select the My Documents Folder check box.

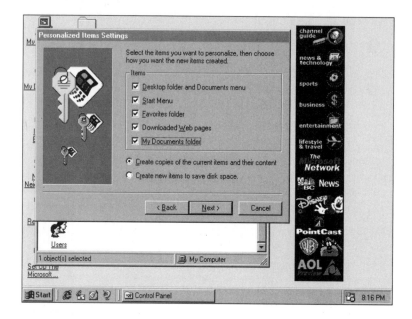

7 Click the Create New Items To Save Disk Space option, and then click Next.

The new user profile will start with the default Windows 98 settings.

8 Click Finish.

The wizard creates your user profile. A message prompting you to restart your computer is displayed. The new profile will not take effect until you restart.

9 Click Yes.

Windows 98 closes and your computer restarts. From now on, when you turn on your computer, you will be prompted to type your username and password.

10 Type your username, and then press TAB.

11 Type your password, and click OK.

Windows 98 starts. Any changes you make to the Desktop, Favorites menu, Start menu, and Outlook Express will only be reflected when you log on using your own username. Other members of your household can create their own settings.

Finish the lesson

1 Close all open windows.

2 If you are finished using your computer for now, click the Start button, and then click Shut Down.

The Shut Down Windows dialog box appears.

3 Select the Shut Down option and click OK.

Windows 98 closes and the computer shuts down.

Lesson 10 Quick Reference

To	Do this
Set up your Internet connection	Contact an Internet Service Provider to set up an account. Click the Start button, point to Programs, point to Internet Explorer, and then click Connection Wizard. Click the I Have An Existing Internet Service Through A Local Area Network Or Internet Service Provider (ISP) option. Click Next. Click the Connect Using My Phone Line option. Click Next. Click the Create A New Dial-Up Connection option. Click Next. Type the phone number. Click Next. Type your username and password. Click Next. Click the No option. Click Next. Type a name for your dial-up connection. Click Next. Click the No option. Click Next. Click the No option. Click Next. Select the No option. Click Next. Click Finish.

Using Your Computer at Home 10

Lesson 10 Quick Reference

To	Do this
Set up your Internet mail account	On the taskbar, click the Launch Outlook Express button. Click Tools, and then click Accounts. Click the Add button, and then click Mail. Type your name. Click Next. Type your e-mail address. Click Next. Type the POP server name. Click Next and then type the SMTP server name. Click Next. Type your password. Click Next. Type a name for your e-mail account. Click Next. Click the Connect Using My Phone Line option. Click Next. Click the Use An Existing Dial-Up Connection option. Click the name of the dial-up connection. Click Next. Close the Internet Accounts dialog box.
Connect to the Internet using your modem	Click the My Computer icon. Click the Dial-Up Networking folder. Click the dial-up connection icon for your account. Type your password. Click the Connect button. Click Close. Close the Dial-Up Networking window.
Open your browser and search for a topic	Open your Internet browser. Click the Search button. Click the Choose A Search Engine link. Click a search engine. In the search box, type the keyword or keywords. Click Search. Click Yes. On the Search bar, click the Close button.
Run a video clip	Click the My Computer icon. Click the drive C icon. Click the folder where the video file is saved. Click the video file.
Record and play a sound message	Click the Start button, point to Programs, point to Accessories, point to Entertainment, and then click Sound Recorder. Click the Record button. Say your message into your microphone. Click the Stop button. Click the Play button.

Lesson 10 Quick Reference

To	Do this	Button
Save a sound message	Be sure that the sound file is open in Sound Recorder. On the File menu, click Save As. Click the drive and folder in which you want the file to be saved. In the File Name box, type the name of the file. Click Save.	
Attach a file to an e-mail message using Outlook Express	On the taskbar, click the Launch Outlook Express button. Click the Compose New Message button. Type the e-mail address. In the message pane, type a message. Click the Insert File button. Locate the file on your hard disk. Click Attach. Click the Send button.	
Create a user profile	Click the Start button, point to Settings, and then click Control Panel. Click Users. Click the New User button. Click Next. Type a password. Click Next. Click the folders and menu options you would like to personalize. Click the Create New Items To Save Disk Space option. Click Next. Click Finish. Click Yes to reboot your computer. Type your username and password.	

Review & Practice

**ESTIMATED
TIME
20 min.**

You will review and practice how to:

✔ *Start Web TV and search for television programs.*

✔ *Watch television programs on your computer.*

✔ *Use a secondary monitor to display more than one program at the same time.*

✔ *Install and use new hardware.*

✔ *Attach files to an e-mail message.*

Before you complete this book, you can practice the skills you learned in Part 4 by working through this Review & Practice section. You will use Microsoft Windows 98 features and new hardware to watch television, play games, and attach files to e-mail messages.

Scenario

You and your partner have combined efforts to produce a television advertising campaign for Mightyflight Toys. The product, a flight simulator computer game, will run during kids' programs today and tomorrow. In addition to the campaign, you go home and play the game and then log on to the Internet to find more pictures and sounds clips that might be useful in future marketing materials.

Step 1:   **Monitor Television Programs While You Work**

You need to monitor the advertisements that are being shown on television today to make sure the networks placed them correctly. You get a reminder when the first show is about to start. You maximize the television window on your second monitor to keep an eye on where the advertisements are placed during the commercial breaks.

1. Start Web TV.
2. Search for kids' television programs playing today, and then sort them by time.
3. Set a reminder for a program that will play in approximately two hours.
4. Select a program from the children's programming list that is currently playing.
5. Drag the television window to your secondary monitor.

For more information about	See
Starting Web TV	Lesson 9
Searching for television programs by category	Lesson 9
Setting reminders for television programs	Lesson 9
Watching a television program on your computer	Lesson 9
Moving a window to the secondary monitor	Lesson 8

Step 2:   **Use New Hardware to Play Games**

After watching kids' programs and advertising all day, you go home with the strong desire to play games. You purchased new hardware, including a DVD drive and a flight controller, and will now install them so that you can run a flight simulator game.

1. Insert a DVD game disc into the DVD drive.
2. Plug a USB ready flight controller in the USB port.
3. Unplug the flight controller, and then plug in a joystick.
4. Start a DVD game, and then play the game with your new hardware.

For more information about	See
Using DVD drives	Lesson 8
Installing USB ready hardware	Lesson 8
Enhancing game performance with Windows 98 improvements	Lesson 10

Step 3: **Communicate over the Internet from Your Home**

You decide to spend some of your recreational time at home browsing the World Wide Web for clip art that might be useful to you or your friends.

1. Open your browser window, and then open the Search pane for your preferred search engine.

2. Search for **clip art** on the World Wide Web. There are many archives on the subject. Open the first clip art Web page that looks interesting to you.

3. Compose a message to a friend, and then attach the clip art file you found and saved. Send the message.

For more information about	See
Searching for Web pages on a particular topic	Lesson 10
Attaching a file to an e-mail message	Lesson 10

Finish the Review & Practice

1. To continue to the next lesson, close any open windows or programs.

2. Return the power management and accessibility settings to your preferred settings.

3. If you are finished using your computer for now, click the Start button, and then click Shut Down.

4. Select the Shut Down option, and click OK. The Windows 98 logo appears as the computer shuts down.

A

Matching the Exercises

Microsoft Windows 98 has many optional settings that can affect either the screen display or the operation of certain functions. Some exercise steps, therefore, might not produce exactly the same result on your screen as is shown in this book. If you do not get the outcome described in the lesson, you can use this appendix to determine whether the options you have selected are the same options used in this book.

important

Each computer system is configured with different hardware and software; therefore, your screen display of icons, folders, and menu options might not exactly match the illustrations in this book. These system differences should not interfere with your ability to perform the exercises in the book.

Installing Windows 98 Components

The exercises in this book assume that a "Typical" setup was used to install Windows 98 on your computer.

If you are missing a component, such as an accessory, you can easily add it. If the component is necessary to complete an exercise, the exercise will help guide you to install or add the component.

Using the Default Windows 98 Settings

In Windows 98, it is easy to configure your Desktop to suit your working style and preferences. However, the exercises and corresponding illustrations in this book assume that all Windows options are at their default settings. If you change option settings while working through the exercises, you will restore the default settings by the end of a lesson.

You can easily change your Windows 98 options to match the illustrations in the exercises by following these steps.

Display or hide the toolbar

You can show or hide the toolbar in most windows, including My Computer and Windows Explorer. The toolbar setting can be different for each window that you open. You can display or hide the toolbar on your screen as appropriate to match the illustrations in this book.

1   In the window, click the View menu.

When there is a checkmark next to the Toolbar command, the toolbar is displayed; if there is no checkmark, the toolbar is hidden.

2   On the View menu, click Toolbar to display or hide the toolbar.

Change window sizes

If the size of your window is different from that shown in the illustrations in the exercises, you can adjust the window.

1   Position the mouse pointer on any edge or corner of the window until the mouse pointer changes to a double-headed arrow.

2   Drag the edge or corner of the window to make the window smaller or larger.

You can change the window size horizontally by dragging a side edge or vertically by dragging the top or bottom; you can simultaneously change the height and the width of a window by dragging a corner.

Restore window sizes

If a window fills the entire screen and you want to see other parts of the Desktop, you can restore the window to its previous size.

Restore

❶   On the taskbar, click the window name button to make it the active window.

❷   In the upper-right corner of the maximized window, click the Restore button.

The window is restored to its previous, smaller size.

Change views

If the way files appear in a window are different from the illustrations in this book, you can easily change the view. The views can be different for each window you open.

●   In the window, click the View menu, and then click the view you want.

The Large Icons view and Small Icons view display graphical symbols for the files. The List view displays a list of the files, and the Details view displays a list along with such details as the file type and the date the file was created or modified.

Arrange icons on the Desktop

If your Desktop icons are jumbled or in a different order from what you want to see, you can arrange them. In the following exercise, you use the AutoArrange command to arrange Desktop icons, and then you arrange the icons by name.

❶   Right-click a blank area on the Desktop.

❷   On the shortcut menu, point to Arrange Icons, and then click AutoArrange.

The icons are aligned in a horizontal and vertical format on the left side of your Desktop.

❸   Right-click a blank area on the Desktop again.

❹   On the shortcut menu, point to Arrange Icons, and then click By Name.

After the default Windows icons on your Desktop, the icons are first arranged by file type, and then in alphabetical order.

Arrange icons in a window

If the icons in a window are jumbled or in a different order from what you want to see, you can arrange them. The icons for each window that you open can have a different arrangement.

 In the window, click the View menu, point to Arrange Icons, and then click AutoArrange.

The icons are aligned horizontally at the top of the window.

 On the View menu, point to Arrange Icons again, and then click By Name.

The icons are first arranged by file type and then in alphabetical order.

Open cascading My Computer windows

By default, a new window opens every time you open a new folder. However, you can set up your computer so that you can browse through folders using a single window. This book assumes that you have not changed the default setting. If you would like to change the default setting, complete the following steps.

 Double-click the My Computer icon.

In the My Computer window, on the View menu, click Folder Options.

The Options dialog box appears.

Be sure that the General tab is active, and then select the Custom option and click Settings. Under the Browser Folders As Follows section, click Open Each Folder In The Same Window.

Click OK.

B

Installing Windows 98

This appendix presents information on installing Microsoft Windows 98. You can install Windows 98 on either a blank hard disk or <u>as an upgrade to</u> Windows 3.1 or Windows 95. After you install Windows 98, you might need to set up your printer. You will find steps for this task at the end of this appendix.

Preparing your computer for Windows 98

Before you install Windows 98, you should make sure your computer meets the minimum requirements. If you are upgrading your computer at work, you should back up your work files to the network or to a backup device. If you are upgrading your computer at home, you should back up your files to a backup device.

Hardware required

To run Windows 98, your computer must have at least the following:

- An Intel 486 DX166MHz or Pentium microprocessor chip *(Pentium II)*
- 16 MB of memory minimum (32 MB is recommended) *(64MB)*
- A hard drive with at least 125 MB free storage space *(6.82 GB)*
- A CD-ROM drive or a 3.5-inch high-density floppy disk drive *(13x min 32x max)*
- A standard (VGA) display adapter with a compatible monitor *(n Vidia 4 MB*
- A mouse or other compatible pointing device *(MS Intell Point)   AGP Graphics)*
- A modem if you plan to connect to an Internet Service Provider *Telepath Modem*
- A network card if you plan to connect to a network

Optional Hardware

To use certain features of Windows 98, you will need the following hardware:

- Sound card with speakers or headphones
- DVD Drive and DVD decoder card or software
- Scanner or digital camera
- TV tuner card

Before you install Windows 98

If you are installing Windows 98 on a blank hard drive, you do not need to complete these steps.

After you have verified that your hardware meets the requirements, you should complete the following steps:

Back up all of your important files. If you are at work and use a network, you might be able to back up your files to the network. If you are at home, you need to back up your files to a backup device, such as a ZIP drive, JAZ drive, or an external hard drive. *Tape backup Sea Gate*

Note your hardware settings. To do this, you can print the autoexec.bat and config.sys files or save them to a floppy disk. You can also view your hardware settings from the Main program group in Windows 3.1 or the My Computer Properties window in Windows 95. For additional information, refer to your Windows 3.1 or Windows 95 user guides.

Read any ReadMe files that are on the Windows 98 CD-ROM. These files contain important information about installing Windows 98. You might want to read the documentation that came with your copy of Windows 98 for additional information.

Installing Windows 98

There are two Windows 98 packages available for purchase. One is a Full Install package that you use if you are installing Windows 98 on a blank hard disk. The other is an Upgrade Install package. You use the Upgrade package if you are upgrading your operating system from Windows 3.1 or Windows 95. You can also use the Full Install package if you are upgrading from Windows 3.1 or Windows 95. However, you cannot load the Upgrade Install on a blank or freshly formatted hard disk.

After you start the installation, the setup program will guide you through the following Setup Wizard steps:

- Detecting the hardware you have installed on your computer system and asking you specific configuration questions about your computer system and about how you want Windows 98 to be set up
- Decompressing and copying Windows 98 program files from the CD-ROM to your hard disk
- Restarting and configuring Windows 98 for use

Install Windows 98 on a blank hard disk

If you would like to install in the cleanest possible environment, you can reformat your hard drive and install Microsoft Windows 98 on a blank hard disk. You must have your CD-ROM drivers loaded on the newly formatted drive. If you need assistance for installing these drivers, contact your CD-ROM drive manufacturer.

1 After your CD-ROM drivers are loaded, insert your Windows 98 CD-ROM in the CD-ROM drive of your computer.

2 At the MS-DOS prompt, type the drive letter of your CD-ROM drive, and then type **\setup.exe**. For example, type **d:\setup.exe** and then press ENTER.

Windows 98 Setup starts. The Welcome To Windows 98 dialog box appears.

3 Click Continue.

4 Click OK.

5 Read the License Agreement. Select the I Accept The Agreement option, and then click Next.

Your acceptance of the license agreement is recorded, and a request for the product identification number appears.

6 Type your product identification number, and then click Next.

You can find the product identification number on the front of the Windows 98 User Guide or on the back of your Windows 98 CD-ROM case.

7 Verify that the network identification information for your computer is correct, and then click Next.

Unless you know that network conditions have changed, you should accept the default settings.

8 Click your country or region, and then click Next.

Microsoft stores update and support information at multiple sites around the world. Your selection of a country or region allows Windows 98 to determine the most efficient and closest Web site to your location. This way, if you need to download future updates, they will be processed more quickly.

9 Click Next to create a startup disk.

You will use the startup disk to start Windows 98 in the event of a hardware or software failure.

10 Label a floppy disk "Windows 98 Startup Disk," and then insert the disk into your floppy disk drive. Click OK.

The files necessary to start Windows 98 in the event of a problem are copied onto the floppy disk.

11 Click OK, and then click Next to start copying the files.

The Windows 98 Setup program collects information about your computer. It then copies the files needed to run Windows 98 onto your hard disk. This process can take several minutes. In the meantime, introductory information about Windows 98 appears on the screen.

12 Remove the Windows 98 startup disk from your floppy drive, and click OK.

The Windows 98 Setup program closes. Your computer restarts and loads Windows 98 for the first time. This process can take several minutes. The Windows 98 Setup program opens and installs software needed to run your hardware.

Depending on your computer's current setup, you might have to restart your computer twice in order to complete the Windows 98 setup process.

13 If you are working on a network, an Enter Network Password dialog box appears. Type your current password and, if necessary, your username in the dialog box, and click OK.

If you have not previously used a password, you will not see this dialog box.

14 Close the Welcome To Windows 98 dialog box.

Install Windows 98 over Windows 3.1

If your computer is currently running Microsoft Windows 3.1 or Windows for Workgroups 3.11, you can install Windows 98 as an upgrade. Most of the settings created for hardware and networking will be copied into the new version. Programs such as a word processing or spreadsheet program should not be affected by the upgrade.

❶ Close any open windows. Insert the Windows 98 CD-ROM in your CD-ROM drive.

❷ In the Program Manager window, click File, and then click Run.

The Run dialog box appears.

❸ Type the drive letter of your CD-ROM drive, and then type **\setup.exe**. For example, type **d:\setup.exe** and then press ENTER.

Windows 98 Setup starts. The Welcome To Windows 98 dialog box appears.

❹ Click Continue.

❺ Click OK.

❻ Read the License Agreement. Select the I Accept The Agreement option, and then click Next.

Your acceptance of the license agreement is recorded, and a request for the product identification number appears.

❼ Type your product identification number, and then click Next.

You can find the product identification number on the front of the Windows 98 User Guide or on the back of the Microsoft Windows 98 CD-ROM case.

❽ Verify that the network identification information for your computer is correct, and then click Next.

Unless you know that network conditions have changed, you should accept the default settings.

❾ Click your country or region, and then click Next.

Microsoft stores update and support information at multiple sites around the world. Your selection of a country or region allows Windows 98 to determine the most efficient and closest Web site to your location. This way, if you need to download future updates, they will be processed more quickly.

❿ Click Next to create a startup disk.

You will use the startup disk to start Windows 98 in the event of a hardware or software failure.

⓫ Label a floppy disk "Windows 98 Startup Disk," and then insert the disk into your floppy disk drive. Click OK.

The files necessary to start Windows 98 in the event of a problem are copied onto the floppy disk.

⓬ Click OK, and then click Next to start copying files.

The Windows 98 Setup program collects information about your computer. It then copies the files needed to run Windows 98 onto your hard disk. This process can take several minutes. In the meantime, introductory information about Windows 98 appears on the screen.

⓭ Remove the Windows 98 startup disk from your floppy drive, and click OK.

The Windows 98 Setup program closes. Your computer restarts and loads Windows 98 for the first time. This process can take several minutes. The Windows 98 Setup program opens and installs software needed to run your hardware.

Depending on your computer's current setup, you might have to restart your computer twice in order to complete the Windows 98 setup process.

⓮ If you are working on a network, an Enter Network Password dialog box appears. Type your current password and, if necessary, your username in the dialog box, and click OK.

If you have not previously used a password, this dialog box will not appear.

⓯ Close the Welcome To Windows 98 dialog box.

Install Windows 98 over Windows 95

If your computer is currently running Microsoft Windows 95, you can install Windows 98 as an upgrade. Most of the settings created for hardware and networking will be copied into the new version. Programs such as a word processing or spreadsheet program should not be affected by the upgrade.

❶ Close any open windows. Insert the Windows 98 CD-ROM in your CD-ROM drive.

❷ Double-click the My Computer icon, and then double-click your CD-ROM drive.

The contents of the Windows 98 CD-ROM are displayed.

❸ Double-click Setup.

Windows 98 Setup starts. The Welcome To Windows 98 dialog box appears.

❹ Click Continue.

❺ Click OK.

❻ Read the License Agreement. Select the I Accept The Agreement option, and then click Next.

Your acceptance of the license agreement is recorded, and a request for the product identification number appears.

❼ Type your product identification number, and then click Next.

You can find the product identification number on the front of the Windows 98 User Guide or the back of your Windows 98 CD-ROM case.

8 Verify that the network identification information for your computer is correct, and then click Next.

The network identification information text is copied from your Windows 95 installation. Unless you know network conditions have changed, you should accept the default settings.

9 Click your country or region, and then click Next.

Microsoft stores update and support information at multiple sites around the world. Your selection of a country or region allows Windows 98 to determine the most efficient and closest Web site to your location. This way, if you need to download future updates, they will be processed more quickly.

10 Click Next to create a startup disk.

You will use the startup disk to start Windows 98 in the event of a hardware or software failure.

11 Label a floppy disk "Windows 98 Startup Disk," and then insert the disk into your floppy disk drive. Click OK.

The files necessary to start Windows 98 in the event of a problem are copied onto the floppy disk.

12 Click OK, and then click Next to start copying files.

The Windows 98 Setup program collects information about your computer. It then copies the files needed to run Windows 98 onto your hard disk. This process can take several minutes. In the meantime, introductory information about Windows 98 appears on the screen.

13 Remove the Windows 98 startup disk from your floppy drive, and click OK.

The Windows 98 Setup program closes. Your computer restarts and loads Windows 98 for the first time. This process can take several minutes. The Windows 98 Setup program opens and installs software needed to run your hardware.

Depending on your computer's current setup, you might have to restart your computer twice in order to complete the Windows 98 setup process.

14 If you are working on a network or if you were using profiles in Microsoft Windows 95, an Enter Network Password dialog box appears. Type your current password and, if necessary, your username in the dialog box, and click OK.

If you have not previously used a password, you will not see this dialog box.

15 Close the Welcome To Windows 98 dialog box.

After Installation

After you have installed Windows 98, you need to install your printer, install any software programs you may want, and setup your Internet connection. The following section will cover how to install your printer. To install software programs, see the documentation that is packaged with the software. To setup your Internet connection, see Lesson 10, "Using Your Computer at Home."

Install a new printer

During initial installation, Windows 98 identifies and installs the necessary software and drivers for printers connected to your computer. However, you can install a new printer without running Windows 98 Setup again.

❶ Click the Start button, click Settings, and then click Printers.

The Printers window opens.

❷ Click Add Printer.

The Add Printer Wizard dialog box appears.

❸ Click Next.

You can add either a network or a local printer. A local printer is connected directly to the back of your computer whereas a network printer is available only over a computer network.

❹ Click the Local Printer option, and then click Next. If you chose the network printer option, skip to the "Install a network printer" exercise.

Windows 98 includes drivers and software for hundreds of printers currently on the market.

❺ Locate your printer manufacturer and printer name in the list provided. If you cannot find either the manufacturer or specific printer name, click the Have Disk button. Insert the printer manufacturer's installation disk in your floppy drive, and click OK. Select your printer, and then click Next.

Generally, a local printer is attached to the LPT1 port. If you are installing a network printer, ask your system administrator for the correct port.

❻ Select the port you want to use with the new printer, and then click Next.

You select a printer by name when you send a print job. Therefore, you should select names for your printers that uniquely identify them. For example, if you have both a LaserJet and an InkJet, you could name them "LaserJet" and "InkJet."

7 Type the printer name, and then click Next.

You have the option of printing a test page to ensure that the new printer is set up correctly. If the printer is attached to your computer (or network), it is recommended that you print a test page.

8 Insert the Windows 98 CD-ROM into your CD-ROM drive. Click Yes, and then click Finish.

Printer files are copied from the installation CD-ROM to your hard disk. A test page is sent to the printer and the Add Printer Wizard closes.

9 A dialog box appears asking Did the Test Page Print Correctly? Click yes.

10 Close the Printers window.

Install a network Printer

1 Click the Start button, click Settings, and then click Printers.

The Printers window opens.

2 Click the Add Printer icon.

The Add Printer Wizard dialog box appears.

3 Click Next.

4 Click the Network printer option and then click Next.

You will be asked for the Network path or the queue name for the network printer. If you don't have this information, ask your system administrator.

5 Type the path or queue name of the printer and then click Next.

You select a printer by name when you send a print job. Most network printers are named by the system administrator. If you don't know the name, ask you system administrator.

6 Type the printer name.

7 To set the printer as your default printer, click the Yes option and then click Next.

8 Be sure that the Yes option to print a test page is selected and then click Finish.

The drivers for the printer are installed on your computer and a test page is printed. The Add Printer Wizard dialog box closes.

9 A dialog box appears asking if the test page printed correctly. Click Yes.

10 Close the Printers window.

Use tutorials to learn about Windows 98

Windows 98 includes brief tutorial programs designed to introduce first-time users to basic computing, provide step-by-step lessons for new Windows users, and provide highlights about Windows 98 for experienced Windows users.

1 Click the Start button, point to Programs, point to Accessories, point to System Tools, and then click Welcome To Windows.

The Welcome To Windows 98 dialog box appears.

2 Click the Discover Windows 98 link.

The Discover Windows 98 program starts.

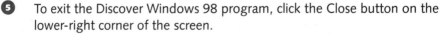

3 Click the Computer Essentials link.

The Computer Essentials tutorial starts. A topic menu appears on the left side of the monitor.

4 Follow the tutorial directions. To exit the tutorial before completion and return to the main menu of the Discover Windows 98 program, click the Contents link at the bottom of the topic menu.

5 To exit the Discover Windows 98 program, click the Close button on the lower-right corner of the screen.

A message asking if you're sure you want to quit Discover Windows 98 is displayed.

6 Click Yes, and then close the Welcome To Windows 98 dialog box.

Register your copy of Windows 98

After you have installed Windows 98 on your computer, you need to register your copy with Microsoft so you can receive technical support, use the Windows Update feature, and receive any notices of new products. To register you need to have an active Internet connection.

❶ Click the Start button, point to Programs, point to Accessories, point to System Tools, and then click Welcome to Windows 98.

The Welcome to Windows 98 dialog box appears.

❷ Click Register Now.

The Microsoft Window 98 Registration wizard appears.

❸ Click Next.

The wizard checks to see if you have an Internet connection.

❹ Click Next.

You are asked to enter information about the product owner.

❺ Click the Home option if you are using Windows 98 at home.

If you are using Windows 98 at work, click the work option.

❻ In the First Name and Middle initial field, type your first name and middle initial and press TAB.

❼ In the last name field, type your last name and then click next.

You are asked to enter your address and phone number information.

❽ In the address field, type your address and press TAB.

❾ If you have additional address information such as an apartment number, type the information and press TAB.

❿ In the city field, type the name of your city and press TAB.

⓫ Type the state or province you live in and press TAB.

⓬ Type your zip code and press TAB.

⓭ Type your phone number and press TAB.

⓮ Type you email address and click Next.

⓯ Type the store name where you bought Windows 98.

⓰ Click the yes option if you want to receive non-Microsoft products and services and then click Next.

You will see an inventory of the hardware that is on your computer.

⑰   Click the yes option if you want to send the inventory list with your registration and then click Next.

You should see a product number in the middle of the dialog box. Write this number down and keep it in a safe place. You might need it if you call Technical Support.

⑱   Click Register.

Your registration is sent to Microsoft.

⑲   Click Finish.

⑳   Close the Welcome to Windows 98 window.

Install the Sound Recorder Program

Before you can record sounds, you must install the Sound Recorder from the Windows 98 CD-ROM.

❶   Click the Start button, point to Settings and then click Control Panel.

The Control Panel window opens.

❷   Click the Add Remove Programs icon.

The Add/Remove Programs Properties dialog box appears.

❸   Click the Windows Setup tab.

The Windows Setup program searches your computer for programs already installed.

❹   Click Multimedia and then click Details.

The Multimedia dialog box appears.

❺   Select the Sound Recorder check box and click OK.

❻   Click OK.

The Sound Recorder program files are installed on your computer.

❼   Close the Control Panel window.

Index

A

B

C

Catapult, Inc. & Microsoft Press

Microsoft Windows 98 Step by Step has been created by the professional trainers and writers at Catapult, Inc., to the exacting standards you've come to expect from Microsoft Press. Together, we are pleased to present this self-paced training guide, which you can use individually or as part of a class.

Catapult, Inc. is a software training company with years of experience in PC and Macintosh instruction. Catapult's exclusive Performance-Based Training system is available in Catapult training centers across North America and at customer sites. Based on the principles of adult learning, Performance-Based Training ensures that students leave the classroom with confidence and the ability to apply skills to real-world scenarios. *Microsoft Windows 98 Step by Step* incorporates Catapult's training expertise to ensure that you'll receive the maximum return on your training time. You'll focus on the skills that can increase your productivity the most while working at your own pace and convenience.

Microsoft Press is the book publishing division of Microsoft Corporation. The leading publisher of information about Microsoft products and services, Microsoft Press is dedicated to providing the highest quality computer books and multimedia training and reference tools that make using Microsoft software easier, more enjoyable, and more productive.

Microsoft Press has titles to help everyone—from new users to seasoned developers—

Step by Step Series
Self-paced tutorials for classroom instruction or individualized study

Starts Here™ Series
Interactive instruction on CD-ROM that helps students learn by doing

Field Guide Series
Concise, task-oriented A–Z references for quick, easy answers— anywhere

Official Series
Timely books on a wide variety of Internet topics geared for advanced users

All User Training   All User Reference

Quick Course® Series
Fast, to-the-point instruction for new users

At a Glance Series
Quick visual guides for task-oriented instruction

Select Editions Series
A comprehensive curriculum alternative to standard documentation books

start faster and go farther!

The wide selection of books and CD-ROMs published by Microsoft Press contain something for every level of user and every area of interest, from just-in-time online training tools to development tools for professional programmers. Look for them at your bookstore or computer store today!

Professional Select Editions Series
Advanced titles geared for the system administrator or technical support career path

Microsoft Certified Professional Training
The Microsoft Official Curriculum for certification exams

Best Practices Series
Candid accounts of the new movement in software development

Microsoft Programming Series
The foundations of software development

Professional   Developers

Strategic Technology Series
Easy-to-read overviews for decision makers

Microsoft Press® Interactive
Integrated multimedia courseware for all levels

Microsoft Professional Editions
Technical information straight from the source

Solution Developer Series
Comprehensive titles for intermediate to advanced developers

Microsoft® Press

mspress.microsoft.com

Keep things **running** smoothly around the **Office.**

These are *the* answer books for business users of Microsoft Office 97 applications. They are packed with everything from quick, clear instructions for new users to comprehensive answers for power users. The Microsoft Press® *Running* series features authoritative handbooks you'll keep by your computer and use every day.

Running Microsoft® Excel 97
Mark Dodge, Chris Kinata, and Craig Stinson
U.S.A. $39.95   ($54.95 Canada)
ISBN 1-57231-321-8

Running Microsoft® Word 97
Russell Borland
U.S.A. $39.95   ($53.95 Canada)
ISBN 1-57231-320-X

Running Microsoft® PowerPoint® 97
Stephen W. Sagman
U.S.A. $29.95   ($39.95 Canada)
ISBN 1-57231-324-2

Running Microsoft® Access 97
John L. Viescas
U.S.A. $39.95   ($54.95 Canada)
ISBN 1-57231-323-4

Running Microsoft® Office 97
Michael Halvorson and Michael Young
U.S.A. $39.95   ($53.95 Canada)
ISBN 1-57231-322-6

***Microsoft* Press**

Take productivity in stride.

Microsoft Press® *Step by Step* books provide quick and easy self-paced training that will help you learn to use the powerful word processor, spreadsheet, database, desktop information manager, and presentation applications of Microsoft Office 97, both individually and together. Prepared by the professional trainers at Catapult, Inc., and Perspection, Inc., these books present easy-to-follow lessons with clear objectives, real-world business examples, and numerous screen shots and illustrations. Each book contains approximately eight hours of instruction. Put Microsoft's Office 97 applications to work today, *Step by Step*.

Microsoft® Excel 97 Step by Step
U.S.A. $29.95   ($39.95 Canada)
ISBN 1-57231-314-5

Microsoft® Word 97 Step by Step
U.S.A. $29.95   ($39.95 Canada)
ISBN 1-57231-313-7

Microsoft® PowerPoint® 97
 Step by Step
U.S.A. $29.95   ($39.95 Canada)
ISBN 1-57231-315-3

Microsoft® Outlook™ 97 Step by Step
U.S.A. $29.99   ($39.99 Canada)
ISBN 1-57231-382-X

Microsoft® Access 97 Step by Step
U.S.A. $29.95   ($39.95 Canada)
ISBN 1-57231-316-1

Microsoft® Office 97 Integration
 Step by Step
U.S.A. $29.95   ($39.95 Canada)
ISBN 1-57231-317-X

The
Microsoft®
Windows 98
Step by Step CD-ROM

The enclosed CD-ROM contains timesaving, ready-to-use practice files that complement the lessons in this book as well as a demonstration of the Microsoft Windows 98 Starts Here interactive training product. To use the CD, you'll need the Windows 98 operating system.

Before you begin the Step by Step lessons, read the "Using the Microsoft Windows 98 Step by Step CD-ROM" section of this book. There you'll find detailed information about the contents of the CD and easy instructions about how to install the files on your computer's hard disk.

Please take a few moments to read the License Agreement on the previous page before using the enclosed CD.

Register your Microsoft Press® book today, and let us know what you think.

At Microsoft Press, we listen to our customers. We update our books as new releases of software are issued, and we'd like you to tell us the kinds of additional information you'd find most useful in these updates. Your feedback will be considered when we prepare a future edition; plus, when you become a registered owner, you will get Microsoft Press catalogs and exclusive offers on specially priced books.
Thanks!

I used this book as
- ● A way to learn the software
- ● A reference when I needed it
- ● A way to find out about advanced features
- ● Other_____

I purchased this book from
- ● A bookstore
- ● A software store
- ● A direct mail offer
- ● Other_____

I consider myself
- ● A beginner or an occasional computer user
- ● An intermediate-level user with a pretty good grasp of the basics
- ● An advanced user who helps and provides solutions for others
- ● Other_____

I will buy the next edition of the book when it's updated
- ● Definitely
- ● Probably
- ● I will not buy the next edition

The next edition of this book should include the following additional information:
1 •_____
2 •_____
3 •_____
The most useful things about this book are_____
_____
This book would be more helpful if_____
_____
My general impressions of this book are_____

May we contact you regarding your comments? ● Yes ● No
Would you like to receive a Microsoft Press catalog regularly? ● Yes ● No

Name_____
Company (if applicable)_____
Address_____
City_____State_____Zip_____
Daytime phone number (optional) (_____)_____

Please mail back your feedback form—postage free! Fold this form as
described on the other side of this card, or fax this sheet to:
Microsoft Press, Attn: Marketing Department, fax 425-936-7329

NO POSTAGE
NECESSARY
IF MAILED
IN THE
UNITED STATES

BUSINESS REPLY MAIL
FIRST-CLASS MAIL   PERMIT NO. 53   BOTHELL, WA

POSTAGE WILL BE PAID BY ADDRESSEE

MICROSOFT PRESS
MICROSOFT® WINDOWS® 98 STEP BY STEP
PO BOX 3019
BOTHELL WA   98041-9946